Here's what top business and management experts are saying about THE POWER OF APPRECIATION IN BUSINESS:

"In *The Power of Appreciation in Business* Noelle Nelson cuts to the chase and addresses what may be the most critical issue in business - the value of people. Every company gives lip service to the idea that they're in a 'people' business. This book goes beyond talking the talk and provides concrete steps to move your company towards true employee appreciation and the performance, productivity, and profits that come with it. **Bravo! a great and useful book for business leaders.**"

- **Joe Calloway, author of** *Indispensable: How To Become The Company That Your Customers Can't Live Without*

"*The Power of Appreciation in Business* recognizes the engine of any great business: people. Its leadership and management techniques can **raise employee engagement and drive customer satisfaction**. An old but true saying sums up the point of this book: "Long after people forget what you did, they will remember how you made them feel.""

- **Tim Sanders, author of** *The Likeability Factor* and *Love is the Killer App*

"Appreciation plays a huge role in motivating employees to work at high performance levels. Our research has shown 'valuing people' to be the number one differentiating characteristic of a high performing workgroup. When valued for their input, workers will take pride in their job and company they work for. **Dr. Nelson shows business owners and managers how to proactively use appreciation to create a productive and profitable work environment.**"

- **Susan Lucia Annunzio, author of** *Contagious Success* **and the chair and CEO of the Hudson Highland Center for High Perfomance**

"*The Power of Appreciation in Business* shows us how to use the high vibrational energy of appreciation to create a motivated workforce where people perform at their best and enjoy being part of the organization. **Every business can benefit from the practical techniques offered by Dr. Noelle Nelson in this excellent book.**"

- **Jeff Keller, author of** *Attitude is Everything*

THE POWER OF APPRECIATION IN BUSINESS

HOW AN OBSESSION WITH VALUE INCREASES PERFORMANCE, PRODUCTIVITY AND PROFITS

OTHER BOOKS BY NOELLE C. NELSON, PH.D.

A Winning Case

Connecting With Your Client

Winning!

Winner Takes All

Dangerous Relationships

Everyday Miracles

The Power of Appreciation

The Power of Appreciation in Everyday Life

THE POWER OF APPRECIATION IN BUSINESS

HOW AN OBSESSION WITH VALUE INCREASES PERFORMANCE, PRODUCTIVITY AND PROFITS

Noelle C. Nelson, Ph.D.

Malibu, California

Publisher's Cataloging-In-Publication Data
(Prepared by The Donohue Group, Inc.)

Nelson, Noelle C.
  The power of appreciation in business : how an obsession with value increases performance, productivity and profits / by Noelle C. Nelson.

    p. : ill. ; cm.
    Includes bibliographical references.
    ISBN: 0-9768073-1-9

1. Industrial management--United States 2. Personnel management--United States. 3. Success in business--United States. 4. Quality of work life--United States. 5. Employee morale--United States. 6. Customer relations--United States. I. Title.

HD31 .N45 2005
658.314

ISBN 0-9768073-1-9
Copyright © 2005 by Noelle C. Nelson - All rights reserved

Attention corporations, business organizations and conferences: Take 40% off and use our books as fundraisers, premiums, or gifts. Please contact the Publisher:

MindLab Publishing
30765 Pacific Coast Highway, Suite 132
Malibu, CA 90265
info@mindlabpublishing.com

No part of this book may be reproduced, stored in a retrieval system, or transmitted in any form or by any means, electronic, mechanical, photocopying, microfilming, recording or otherwise, without written permission from the Publisher, except for the inclusion of brief quotations in a review.

Library of Congress Control Number: 2005931019

Printed in the United States of America   10 9 8 7 6 5 4 3 2 1

Acknowledgments

There is so much to be grateful for, so much to appreciate, it's difficult to know where to begin. I am profoundly grateful for all those who over the years have shown me the immense value of appreciation and how it truly is a life-changer, a tremendous force for success in all arenas. I wish to thank with applause and fanfare those who were instrumental in the research, development and production of this book for their amazing patience, good humor, terrific work and valuable insights: Russell Bond, Michelle Masamitsu, Diane Rumbaugh.

My heartfelt thanks to the companies who contributed their experiences and the individuals who represented them with grace and enthusiasm: Melanie Jones and Sunny Stone of Southwest Airlines, Richard Van Doreen of See's Candies, Inc., Edward Rifenburg of Ryder Systems, Inc., Joe Angelicola of Professional Cutlery Direct, Lori Hardy of Barkley Evergreen & Partners Public Relations and Ray

Acknowledgments

Pelletier of The Pelletier Group.

For permission to use copyrighted materials, I am grateful to the following: The Jackson Organization, for material from "Employee Recognition and Profitability: Making the Connection." Copyright © 2005 by The Jackson Organization. The Institute of HeartMath ® Research Center, for materials from "The HeartMath Solution," HarperCollins,1999: Imprint: HarperSanFrancisco. Copyright © 1997 – 2005 by Institute of HeartMath ® Research Center.

CONTENTS

PREFACE .... *xiii*

CHAPTER 1
APPRECIATION'S POWER: THE SCIENCE
    What is Appreciation? 1
    Appreciation's Impact on Three Profitability Measures:
        Return on Equity, Return on Assets, and Operating
        Margin 2
    How Appreciation Enhances Your Business's Bottom
        Line. 6
    How Appreciation Works 8
    The Phenomenon of Entrainment 10
    What Are You Entraining at Work? 13
    The Effect of Your Thoughts and Feelings on
        Others 14
    Synchronizing Expectations for Success 15

Contents

The Impact of Appreciation on Your Heart	16
Your Heart's Electromagnetic Field	18
Your Heart's Influence on Others	19
The Impact of Appreciation on Your Brain	21
The Power of Your Expectations	24
How Appreciation Removes Resistance	25
Appreciation: An Obsession with Value	26
A New Paradigm for Business Success	27
How Do I Appreciate?	28

CHAPTER 2
IT ALL STARTS WITH YOU

Appreciation's Driving Force	31
What Does Your Appreciation Meter Read?	32
Shift Your Focus	36
Problem Solving with Appreciation	37
Appreciation Increases Your Mental Effectiveness	39
Be Sincere	41
Acknowledge People	42
Watch Your Talk	45
Walk Your Talk	47
Lead by Example	50
Live Up to Your Promises	52
Create a Culture of Appreciation	54

Contents

    Follow Through 65

CHAPTER 3
EMPLOYEES: THE GREAT DIVIDE

    Appreciation and Job Retention 57
    From High Hopes to Bare Minimum 59
    Appreciate Your Employees' Work 61
    Show Value by Asking Questions 65
    Tell Employees How Their Work Matters 67
    Give Appreciative Feedback 68
    Address Poor Performance Appreciatively 70
    Get Employees Involved 71
    Use Employee Ideas 73
    Celebrate at Every Opportunity 77
    Appreciate Who Your Employees Are 85
    The Workspace 86
    Don't Overstress Good Employees 89
    Value What is of Value to the Employee 92
    Appreciate Grievances 95
    A Genuine Open Door Policy 96
    A Suggestion Box that Works 97
    Encourage training and classes 99
    Share Company Information 100

Appreciation Supports Employee Health and
Well-Being 102

CHAPTER 4
MANAGERS: BETWEEN A ROCK AND A HARD PLACE

Managing People versus Managing Systems 107
Be Your Best to Entrain the Best 109
Don't Ignore the Basics 110
Catch People in the Act of Doing Something Right 114
How to Give Appreciative Comments 116
Be a Part of, Not Apart From 117
Set Your People Up for Success 120
Be a Problem Solver, Not a Problem Creator 122
Value All Your People 124
Appreciative Listening 125
Listening to Employee Grievances 129
Ask for Employee Opinions 133

CHAPTER 5
CUSTOMERS: THE NECESSARY EVIL?

A New Power Dynamic 135
It's All About the Experience 138
Deliver on Your Promises 141
Getting to Know You 145

Contents

    Use Focus Groups 148
    Getting to Know the Corporate Client 152
    Combat the "Us versus Them" Mentality 154
    Reality Check 158
    The Conscious Employee 159
    Train Your Employees to Appreciate 162
    Appreciate Customer Complaints 166
    Cultivate the Customer's Experience 170
    The Customer Is Your Business 174

STAYING IN TOUCH 177

REFERENCES AND RECOMMENDED READING 179

Preface

I have been a clinical psychologist and trial consultant for many years. I have come to my understanding of, and tremendous respect for, the power of appreciation from these two very different perspectives.

As a clinical psychologist, both in my research and working with clients in psychotherapy, I have observed the remarkable mental, emotional and physical benefits of appreciation. But it is in my work as a trial consultant, helping lawyers develop case strategies, that I came to realize the enormous importance of appreciation in business.

For almost two decades, I have had the woeful advantage of seeing the dark side of business: employees--from warehouse workers to CFOs--suing employers; customers of every ilk suing businesses from the smallest Mom and Pop to the mega-giants of industry; companies suing each other for an astonishing array of reasons. But the most common reason, underlying whatever the stated complaint,

Preface

is lack of appreciation.

In some way, the complaining party feels unappreciated, treated as disposable, unimportant, without value--and a lawsuit ensues. The cost to business is astronomical, not just in lawyers' fees and actual dollars awarded in jury verdicts or settlements, but in the time, energy, company manpower and effort spent to represent or defend litigation.

These lawsuits merely highlight what has become "the elephant in the living room" of business, the problem everybody knows about but nobody wants to acknowledge: ***lack of appreciation in the workplace cripples performance, productivity and profitability.***

How? Well, business is all about people. Sure, there's product and manufacturing and other material things, but in the end, it all boils down to people. Whether you're an automobile maker, a manufacturer in China, run a big box store or have a solo accounting practice, with few exceptions, you're dealing with people.

Knowing how to work successfully with people is absolutely critical to your success and the success of your business. And working successfully with people is predicated on one basic principle: How much do you appreciate people? Or, more to the point, how much do you *value* the people who make the product, perform the service,

Preface

manage, sell and buy whatever it is you offer? Appreciation is primarily composed of valuing. Valuing the people in and around your business is a prime determinant of success.

Sounds simple, doesn't it? Sounds like something we all know how to do. So why does the U.S. Department of Labor tell us that the ***number one*** reason people leave their jobs is--lack of appreciation? Why do fully 65 percent of workers polled by Gallup say they didn't receive a single word of praise or recognition in the past year? And why, although customer satisfaction may be good, customer loyalty is not?

Perhaps because we really don't know how to value and appreciate people in a way that will motivate them to perform at their peak, and in turn, increase company profits. Perhaps because we don't know what appreciation is all about, why it works the way it does, and therefore, how to use it most effectively.

Appreciation is not just another word for gratitude. Appreciation isn't just a pleasant acknowledgement of something good. Appreciation is an energy, like gravity, like electricity. Its tremendous impact has been proven ***scientifically*** again and again. Because appreciation is energy, you can harness and apply it to greatly improve the bottom line--the performance, productivity and profitability of your business.

Preface

Some companies have understood and utilized the tremendous power of appreciation to their benefit. Southwest Airlines, Ryder System Inc., See's Candies, Barkley Evergreen & Partners and Professional Cutlery, LLC are companies of varying sizes within different industries that are particularly adept at using appreciation techniques in their businesses. Their experience and insight are quoted throughout the book to further illustrate the real-world hands on use of appreciation.

A workplace without the appropriate appreciation mechanisms in place is a breeding ground for employee stress, apathy, low motivation, lack of company loyalty, poor performance, customer indifference and lawsuits. The dollars lost each day by business because of this workplace malaise is staggering. It comes to an estimated $250 to $300 billion a year! If you want to see the difference appreciation can make to your business, it's time to make a change. This book will show you how.

Noelle C. Nelson

Malibu, 2005

The Power of Appreciation in Business

How an Obsession with Value Increases Performance, Productivity and Profit

CHAPTER 1

APPRECIATION'S POWER: THE SCIENCE

WHAT IS APPRECIATION?

Appreciation is one of the most powerful, yet misunderstood, misused and untapped energies available to us. We're used to thinking of appreciation as just another word for gratitude, an expression of recognition and thanks for a job well done, a service performed, an unexpected kindness. In the business world, appreciation is most often an after-the-fact acknowledgement, sometimes accompanied by a reward, in hopes of continuing a desired behavior.

For example, the "Employee of the Month" award is an after-the-fact acknowledgement of an employee's superior work performance during the preceding month. It is given with the hopes of motivating other employees to strive for the award and thus giving the company the benefit of their superior performance.

And that's nice. It even works, to a degree. But such a milquetoast understanding of appreciation doesn't even begin to tap its true power, the force of nature that it is, and what it can really do in the business environment. For appreciation, you see, is energy with enormous predictable impact-- impact that science proves repeatedly.

APPRECIATION'S IMPACT ON THREE PROFITABILITY MEASURES: RETURN ON EQUITY, RETURN ON ASSETS, AND OPERATING MARGIN

Recent research shows that appreciation in the form of employee recognition, for example, has direct and unmistakable impact on a business's profitability. A study conducted by The Jackson Organization included 26,000 employees at all levels in 31 organizations of varying types and sizes. In addition to other questions, employees were asked to state to what degree they agreed with the question: "My organization recognizes excellence," another way of saying "My organization appreciates me." These responses were statistically analyzed and then compared with three profitability measures: return on equity, return on assets, and operating margin (The Jackson Organization, *Employee Recognition and Profitability: Making the Connection*) .

Appreciation's Power: the Science

As you can see from the graphs on this and the next two pages, the results are dramatic in all three arenas.

Recognition and Return on Equity

Return on Equity is a critical measure that encompasses profitability, asset management and financial leverage. According to the data, companies that effectively recognize excellence [appreciate employee value] enjoyed a return on equity more than three times higher than the return experienced by firms that don't. (The Jackson Organization, Ibid.)

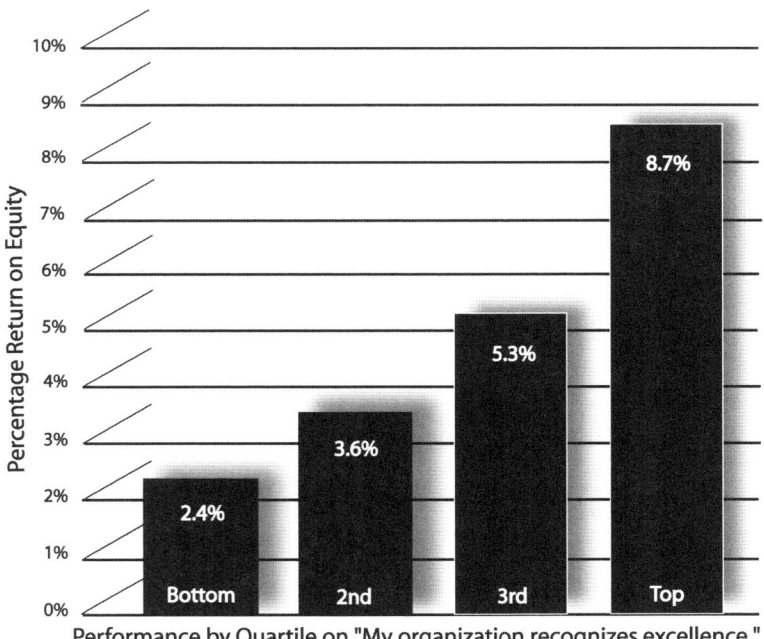

Recognition and Return on Assets

Return on Assets is a measure of a firm's effectiveness in using the assets at hand to generate earnings. According to the data, companies that effectively recognize excellence enjoy a return on assets more than three times higher than the return experienced by firms that don't. (The Jackson Organization, Ibid.)

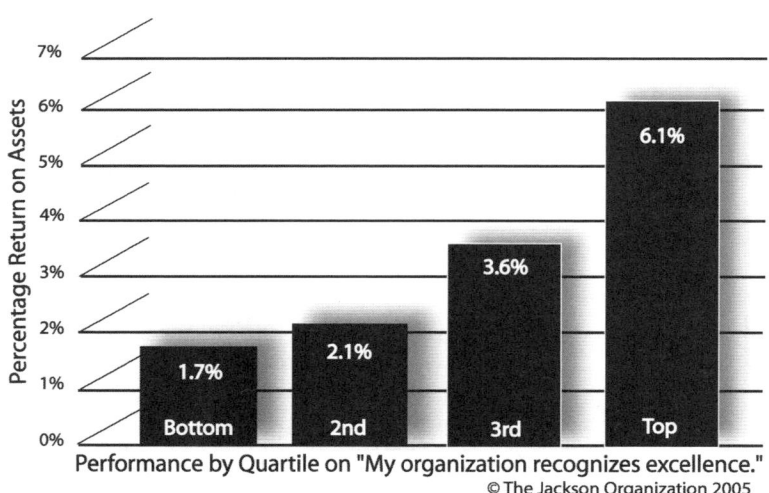

Appreciation's Power: the Science

Recognition and Operating Margin

Operating Margin is another measure of an organization's efficiency. In general, businesses with higher Operating Margins tend to have lower fixed costs and better gross margins. According to the data, companies in the highest quartile of agreement with the statement, "My organization recognizes excellence," reported an Operating Margin of 6.6%, while those in the lowest quartile reported only 1%. (The Jackson Organization, Ibid.)

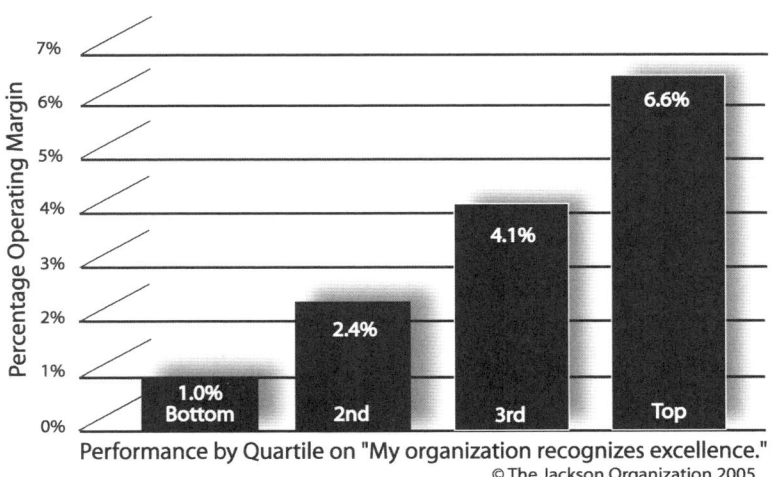

The researchers concluded their study by saying:

"Companies that effectively recognize excellence enjoy a return that is more than triple the return of companies that don't."

HOW APPRECIATION ENHANCES YOUR BUSINESS'S BOTTOM LINE

Appreciation's power derives first from appreciation's ability to synchronize expectations. Synchronization of expectations assures you that what you want (expect) from your employees, your managers or your customers is what they are willing and expect to do for you. Synchronized expectations can create smoother operations and higher profitability. More specifically, expectations synchronized through appreciation lead to:

- increased employee commitment

- greatly reduced employee absenteeism and turnover

- the creation of a better, more reliable product/service

Appreciation's Power: the Science

- product/service elevated from price-driven "commodity" to valued experience

- increased customer loyalty

All of which can considerably enhance your business's bottom line.

Appreciation also propagates a number of valued states of being or valued state of affairs, such as:

- greatly improved communication at all levels

- increased competency of employees and managers

- increased willingness to "go the extra mile"

- enhanced perceived value of your product/service

- increased willingness of employees and managers to learn, change and grow

- increased solution-orientation and adoption of responsibility/accountability

- increased employee motivation and higher morale

- decrease in conflict

- increase in teamwork effectiveness

- increased employee physical and mental well-being

- increased mental acumen and focus

All of which will yield an even more enhanced bottom line.

This is not theory. This is not wishful thinking. This is the scientifically demonstrable impact of appreciation.

HOW APPRECIATION WORKS

So how does appreciation work? What makes appreciation so very powerful? We first have to take a brief look at quantum physics, energy and vibration.

As quantum physics teaches us, everything is first and foremost energy: you, me, this book, the mood you were in this morning, your dog or cat--all of it is just different forms of energy. We, and the world within and around us, are really nothing more than a mass of electrons swirling around that is expressed as different kinds of matter or experiences. Everything is energy first, matter second.

Energy, by definition, is always in motion (it's hard to imagine a swirling mass of electrons that isn't) and that motion is known as a vibration. And since you, me, the book you are holding, the mood you were in this morning are, in their most basic forms, a mass of swirling electrons or energy, we all have a vibration. Vibrations are measured in terms of frequency, or the number of vibrations per second.

The earth, for example, vibrates at 7.5 times per second, a vibration we're hardly, if ever, aware of. Musical tones vibrate at around 16 to 20,000 times per second. These vibrations are much easier to perceive, not only with our ears and brain, which translate these vibrations into sound, but even with our bodies. Anyone who has teenagers in the home knows - musical vibrations will literally rock the walls!

Your brain has a frequency of vibration called a brain wave. Your heart has a frequency of vibration called your heart rhythm. Scientists measure brain waves and heart rhythms routinely, and have found that the impact of appreciation on your heart and brain is profound, as we'll see shortly. Your thoughts, your feelings, your very person all have a frequency of vibration.

Vibration, in this context, isn't something indefinable that's "in the air." Vibration describes the movement of energy, based on the scientific knowledge that energy is the basis of all things, both material and immaterial.

THE PHENOMENON OF ENTRAINMENT

Vibrations match up with or synchronize with other vibrations through a scientific process called "entrainment." One classic scientific demonstration of entrainment is the violin experiment. Two identical violins are placed at opposite ends of a room. A violin string is plucked on one of the violins, whereupon a string on the violin across the room will begin to vibrate at the same note (frequency) as the plucked string – without anybody touching it. The less intense vibration of the second violin has matched up with the more intense vibration of the plucked violin. The second violin's vibration has been pulled along, if you will, into the more intense vibration of the plucked violin. This is entrainment. The stronger and more intense vibration will "entrain" the less intense vibration to synchronize with it.

> Christian Huygens discovered the phenomenon of entrainment quite by accident in the 17th century. Huygens, the inventor of the pendulum clock, had quite a collection of them. One day Huygens was observing his clocks, when he noticed what appeared to be an unusual circumstance. Even though he had not set the

clocks to do so, all of his pendulums were swinging in unison. Puzzled, Huygens then deliberately set the pendulums to swing at different rhythms, yet the clocks soon began to swing once again in perfect synchronization. They all followed the beat set by the pendulum with the strongest rhythm.

Scientists have since observed entrainment in a whole host of phenomena many of which are experienced by all of us at one time or another.

For example, if you walk into a room full of depressed people, you'll find that after a relatively brief period of time, you too will feel depressed. If on the other hand you walk into a room full of happy, laughing people, in short order you'll feel happier yourself. In both cases, you've been entrained. The vibration of an entire roomful of people is generally stronger than your individual vibration. As a result, your vibration will be entrained to their vibration, happy or sad, unless you do something to actively resist it.

<u>Entrainment</u> explains why when you behave in accordance with a strongly focused vibration, you will be responded to in the same way, as long as no resistance is present. For example, if you get angry with someone, the person you are angry at is likely to get angry and defensive in return, even though they may express that anger passively or indirectly. Your strongly focused vibration of anger has

entrained a vibration of anger from the person, even if originally he or she were not feeling angry at all.

Similarly, have you ever noticed how hard it is to stop an argument once it really gets going? That's because one person's vibration of anger matches up with the other person's vibrations of anger, entraining both to create – greater anger. On the other hand, if you respond to a situation by seeking to understand what's going on, the person is likely to make an effort to help you understand. Your strongly focused vibration of "wanting to understand" entrains a vibration from the other person that synchronizes with your "understanding" approach.

As is demonstrated by the violin experiment, vibration aligns with like vibration. The second violin is entrained to vibrate at the same frequency or note as the plucked violin. It will not vibrate at a different frequency. Anger entrains anger. Understanding entrains understanding.

Absent resistance, "like attracts like." Other familiar phrases such as "what goes around, comes around," and "what you give is what you get" are grounded in this scientific reality. Our universe and everything in it are composed of vibrating energy. The energy you give off, whatever that may be, supports and encourages experiences of like energy.

WHAT ARE YOU ENTRAINING AT WORK?

To get the results you want in business, you need to be aware of what you are entraining. Whether you realize it or not, you are already entraining the vibrations of those around you at work by virtue of your position as store owner, CEO, department head, supervisor or manager. The question isn't "Are you the entrainer?" but rather "What are you entraining?"

Let's say you're frustrated with a vendor. You're not getting the materials you need in timely fashion. You've just hung up the phone after yet another round of "Where is it?" "I don't know, I'll have to check with dispatch," when an excited employee comes in with an idea to improve workflow. "Yeah, fine, write something up," you say, hardly listening and already onto the next thing. Unfortunately, you've just entrained an uncaring, unresponsive vibration from your employee, who now probably won't bother pursuing an idea that could have been a valuable contribution to improved workflow. What's worse, the employee is unlikely to enthusiastically suggest other ideas in the future.

Entraining the vibrations that will advance your business is critical to your success. Now granted, this is a very different approach to increasing performance, productivity and profitability from what's taught in business schools. And the whole idea of synchronizing expectations by "matching vibrations" or "entraining" may seem very strange, very out there–until you realize that your vibration is primarily determined simply by what you think and feel.

*Your vibration is made up of
what you think and what you feel.*

The problem is, a lot of us aren't aware of what we're thinking and what we're feeling, much less the direct impact our individual vibrations have on how our world works.

THE EFFECT OF YOUR THOUGHTS AND FEELINGS ON OTHERS

For instance, you may, in the previous example, have been aware of your frustration with the vendor, but how aware were you of the effect of your frustration on your employee?

Let's say you're preoccupied with your day. Your thoughts and feelings are full of the meetings you know lie ahead, that problem in accounting that has yet to be resolved, and the glitch in production no one seems to want to accept responsibility for. As a result, you fail to greet employees as you pass them in the hall. Your failure to acknowledge employees readily matches up with whatever vibration of worthlessness they may have within them, and thereby lead to decreased competence. Your expectation of good work from employees no longer synchronizes with their expectation of respect from you. The result? An "I don't care about you either" attitude from your employees, who now don't put forth the level of productivity or performance you could otherwise expect.

Conversely, if despite your preoccupation with your day, you greet your employees with a smiled "How ya doin'" as you pass them in the hall, that appreciative acknowledgement readily matches up with whatever vibration of value they have within them, leading to increased competence. Your expectation of good work from employees now is synchronized with their expectation of respect from you. The result? An "I care about you too" attitude from your employees who now will perform with greater effort.

SYNCHRONIZING EXPECTATIONS FOR SUCCESS

When you're not aware of the impact of your vibration, your effectiveness is hit or miss. When you know how to use vibration purposefully and deliberately, you can synchronize expectations that directly contribute to your success, whether you're a manager, VP, department head, business owner or CEO.

Synchronizing expectations means you don't have to

demand or force people into behaving the way you want them to. You don't have to argue them into doing something. You're not seducing, manipulating or bribing – none of which ever really work, certainly not for any length of time. You're simply synchronizing their expectations with yours so that they want to work with you to accomplish your goals and want to be there for you in the ways you desire.

When people feel valued, feel that who they are and what they do are of worth, people become willing and eager to cooperate with you. Appreciation entrains appreciation. Your vibration of appreciation of people entrains their vibration of appreciation towards you. It is now possible to easily and smoothly synchronize expectations: the stage has been well set.

THE IMPACT OF APPRECIATION ON YOUR HEART

Within our own bodies, appreciation entrains highly valued states of being.

For example, as shown on the following graphs, scientists have demonstrated that when you think and feel appreciation, your heart rhythm is steady, even and well balanced. When you think and feel anger or fear, you entrain a very different heart rhythm, one that is chaotic or disordered.

Appreciation's Power: the Science

Your Heart on Appreciation

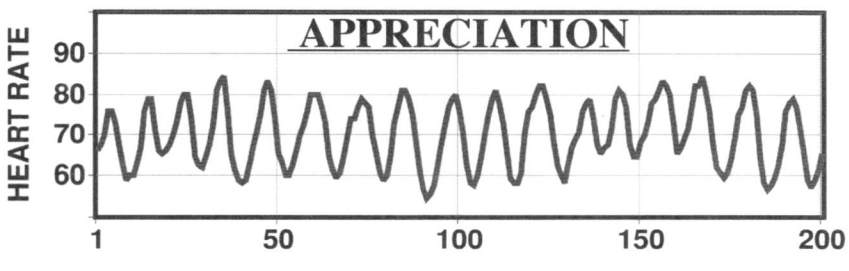

Your Heart on Anger

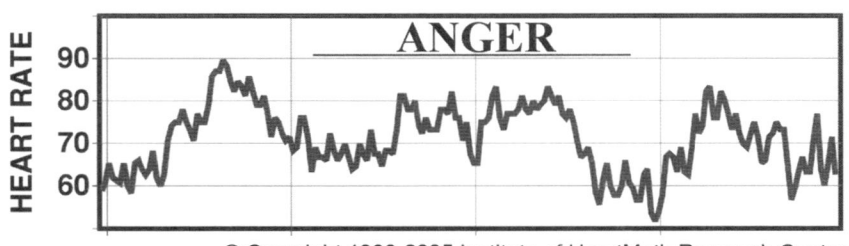

Anger creates a chain reaction in the body: blood vessels constrict, blood pressure rises, which eventually may lead to hypertension and the increased possibility of heart disease and stroke.

Appreciation, on the other hand, entrains harmonious heart rhythms, which in turn support good cardiovascular health, enhance the immune system, help the nervous system function smoothly and improve hormonal balance. Appreciation entrains the synergistic working-together of the whole body, resulting in an overall state of well-being, good energy, and better emotional, mental and physical health (Childre, D. & Martin, H. *The Heartmath Solution*).

YOUR HEART'S ELECTROMAGNETIC FIELD

In the wireless world we live in, cell phones, pagers, iPods, wireless Internet access and all manner of other devices transmit information via electromagnetic fields. So too does the human heart.

The heart's electromagnetic field is tremendously powerful. It can be measured up to eight to 10 feet outside of our bodies.

Appreciation's Power: the Science

The Heart's Electromagnetic Field

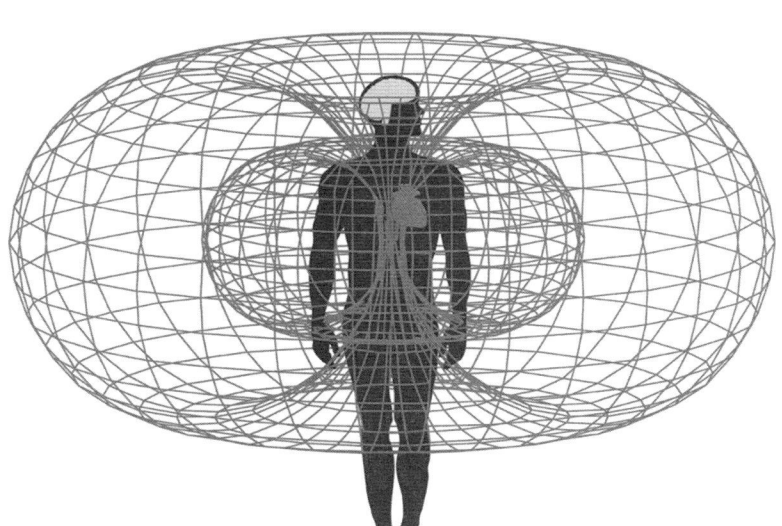

© Copyright Institute of HeartMath

YOUR HEART'S INFLUENCE ON OTHERS

What you are thinking and feeling is transmitted via your heart's electrical energy and shows up in the brain waves of those standing near you.

Signal-averaging techniques were used by the researchers at The Institute of HeartMath Research Center to show that when two people touch, there's a transfer of the electrical energy generated by one person's heart (as represented by the tracings on an ECG) that can be detected in the other person's brain waves (via EEG). *A similar effect is detected when two subjects stand close together, such as in an elevator or in a department store, without touching.* (Childre & Martin, Ibid.)

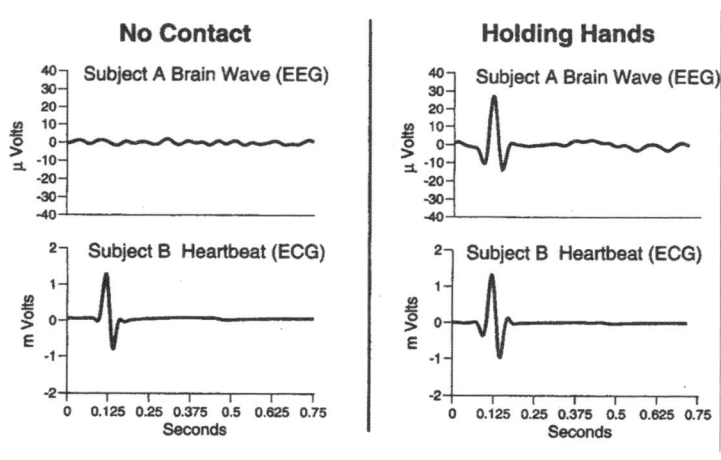

© Copyright 1998-2005 Institute of HeartMath Research Center

Whether you mean to or not, you have an effect on those in physical proximity to you at the most basic electromagnetic level. By virtue of thinking and feeling appreciation, you have a coherence-producing, stress-reducing impact on those around you. Your appreciating entrains a valued state of being from self and others.

Appreciation's Power: the Science

THE IMPACT OF APPRECIATION ON YOUR BRAIN

Appreciation also dramatically affects brain function, which in turn has immediate impact on how your mind works--or doesn't.

Your brain relies on blood flowing to it in order to function properly. Various portions of your brain will function well or poorly depending on whether or not blood is flowing to them.

The SPECT scans of the brain (a neuro-imaging technique) on the following two pages show that when you think and feel appreciation, blood flows readily to your brain, whereas when you are thinking and feeling negative thoughts, blood flow is greatly diminished.

As a result, when you are thinking and feeling appreciation, your brain functions well, firing on all cylinders as it were. Various portions of the brain are properly active, supporting, for example, your ability to be flexible and cooperate readily with others. You have no trouble being motivated and setting goals. Your thoughts are well focused. It's easy for you to switch from one idea to another. Your memory is good. Physically you are coordinated and energized, all of which add up to a very valued state of being indeed.

The Power of Appreciation in Business

Your Brain on Appreciation

SPECT scan measuring blood flow to the brain (the dense areas in white) while thinking and feeling appreciation.

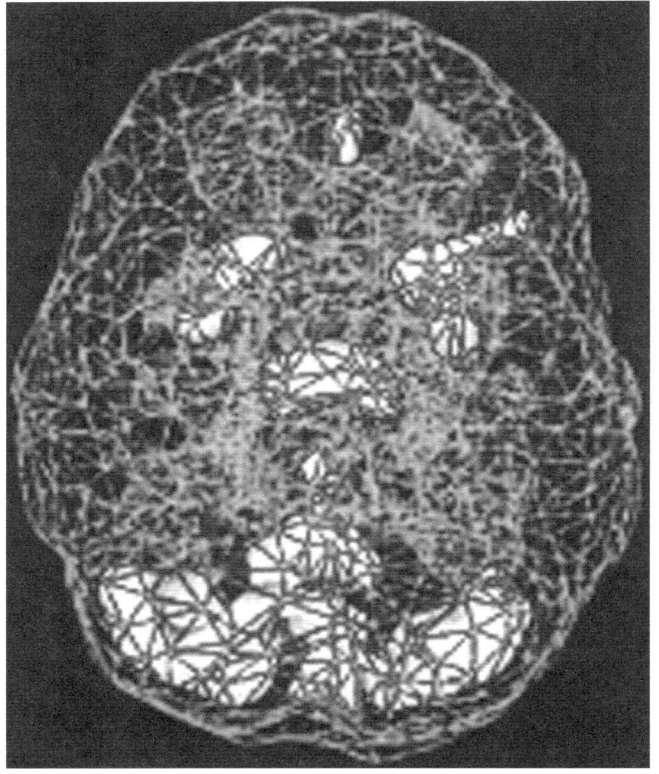

© 2003 Noelle Nelson

Appreciation's Power: the Science

Your Brain on Negativity

SPECT scan measuring blood flow to the brain (the dense areas in white) while thinking and feeling negativity.

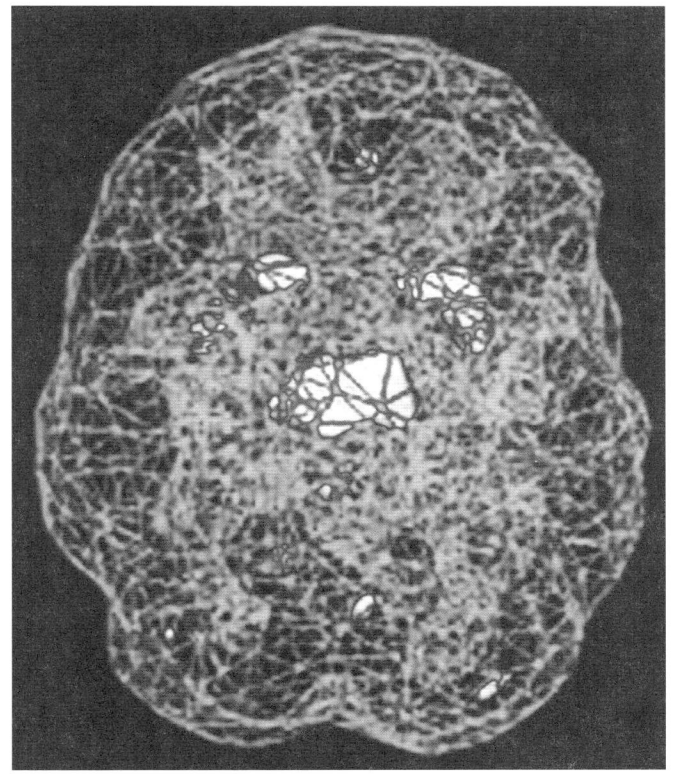

© 2003 Noelle Nelson

The Power of Appreciation in Business

Anger or strong negative thoughts entrain a very different state of being: blood flow to the brain is greatly diminished in many areas. The result is that you experience physical difficulties. Your coordination is impaired. Your emotions become unstable. You may become anxious or fearful for no apparent reason. Your thoughts are confused. Your memory is faulty. You are more susceptible to hostility, inner turmoil and acting in violent ways. As a result, you may feel angry, frustrated, distressed, on edge and depressed--emotions that will lead you to respond to situations in negative and destructive ways. Hardly a valued state of being!

THE POWER OF YOUR EXPECTATIONS

The power of appreciation as an entrainer of vibrations can be used to explain the well-known Pygmalion Effect, also known as the Power of Expectations. In classroom experiments, teachers with high expectations of their students get far better results from those students. Teachers with few expectations of their students have classrooms full of underachieving students. The workplace is no different.

Bosses and managers have expectations of the people they work with, and to a surprising degree, people perform in line with those expectations. Managers with high expectations of the people they supervise see the value of those people, and the manager's vibration of appreciation entrains a vibration of appreciation from them. These workers will now literally seek to demonstrate their value to their manager. Appreciation truly brings out the best in people.

HOW APPRECIATION REMOVES RESISTANCE

Another important vibrational function of appreciation is to remove resistance. In the absence of resistance, all things work together harmoniously. In the workplace, resistance consists of fault-finding, blaming, criticizing, dismissing and ignoring, to name but the most common. A vibration of fault-finding or blaming will most often be matched by an equal vibration of fault-finding or blaming. Your "you did a lousy job on this" is met with "it's not my fault, so-and-so messed up their part of it," and nothing gets resolved.

When you set aside your desire to blame (however justified) and instead look for something to value in the situation, your vibration of appreciation will entrain a corresponding appreciative or valuing vibration. "Your effort on this project was really good. A, B and C came out well. We need to take another look at D, OK?" Since this statement offers no resistant vibration, it will be met with an equally non-resistant vibration, such as "Oh, OK. What do you need me to do?" Removing resistance eliminates a tremendous amount of wasted time, energy and human potential, all of which are a terrible drain on your company's resources.

Removing resistance by appreciating does not deny the presence or existence of the other person's poor performance. It simply takes the focus off fault-finding in the interests of finding good solutions to the problem. A person's poor performance can be dealt with in more productive ways than pointing fingers and blaming.

APPRECIATION: AN OBSESSION WITH VALUE

So we're back to the original question: what is appreciation? Well, it's not Pollyanna, and it's not positive thinking. Pollyanna would imply that one ignores the various flaws and failings of people or products, walking around with an "All is well" attitude when all is most definitely NOT well. Appreciation is a matter of focus, not denial. Positive thinking is a wishful hoping for something in the future. Appreciation is a valuing of something in the immediate here and now. There is nothing wishful or hopeful about it. Appreciation is one of the most reality-based business approaches you can possibly take.

Appreciation is an obsession with value.

The appreciation we've discussed here has little in common with the "Gee thanks," version of appreciation we usually think of.

This is a completely different order of appreciation. This appreciation deliberately, proactively and enthusiastically seeks out the value of someone or something and loudly proclaims that value.

Appreciation in the work environment is determining what someone or something means to you, how it matters to you, and letting that someone know and all others involved know just how important that meaning, that mattering is to you. Appreciation is seeking out, validating and growing the value of someone or something. This is the kind of appreciation people speak of when they say, "Land appreciates, gold appreciates, art appreciates." Appreciation has first and foremost to do with the value of people and things.

A NEW PARADIGM FOR BUSINESS SUCCESS

This way of working with appreciation represents a new paradigm. It is a shift in perspective, a fundamental change in approach, an obsessive search for *value*, for worth, in every situation, in every person. The overriding question becomes: "What is of value here?" The answer is "Something." You may not know what it is at first, but you can safely assume that there is something of value for you to find and once you ask the question, it will be fruitfully answered. There is value in everything and everyone, and the search for it is what makes appreciation a linchpin for success.

HOW DO I APPRECIATE?

What you think and what you feel is what determines your vibration. Appreciation is composed of a certain way of thinking and a certain way of feeling.

The thinking portion of "I appreciate" is to recognize worth and acknowledge value: "I focus my thoughts on your worth, on your value--and because I'm consistently, persistently, intensely thinking of your value and worth and expressing that worth to you – you, in turn, demonstrate your value, your worth to me." Appreciation is about thinking valuing thoughts and everything responds to being valued.

The feeling portion of "I appreciate" is to be genuinely grateful for whatever it is you value. Once you value someone or something, simply let the gratitude flow. Everything responds to gratitude.

There is no need for someone to do something that prompts your appreciation. This new paradigm implies that you are seeking to entrain value regardless of what is in front of you at the moment. Appreciation is a proactive approach, requiring nothing more than your willingness to think a certain way. Since you can always choose what you think, you are in control.

Appreciation's Power: the Science

The following chapters show specifically how to appreciate in four critical areas of business: leadership, employees, managers and customers.

CHAPTER 2

IT ALL STARTS WITH YOU

APPRECIATION'S DRIVING FORCE

When you're in a leadership or management position, whether you're the owner of a Mom-and-Pop grocery store, manager of a Big Box store, supervisor of a warehouse, head of the accounting department, or a Fortune 500 CEO, what you think and what you feel affects every person involved with your company or your department at every level.

You set the tone, you set the pace, and you determine what is going to matter and what isn't. Your vibration is the single most important vibration in your business. The trickle down effect is real. You have enormous vibrational impact.

If you see your products and services as having tremendous

value, your employees or those you supervise will appreciate them in the same way. If you see the people who work with and for you to create that product or service as having tremendous value, those people will want to step up to the plate for you again and again. If you see your customers as having tremendous value, and provide them with an experience matching that value, your customers will appreciate your product or service, and become veritable champions for your company. Your business cannot help but prosper. It's scientific. Like attracts like.

This may seem extremely obvious to you, and you may be thinking, "Well of course I think my product/service is great, and the people who work for me are - well, they're pretty OK. And sure I love my customers; where would I be without them?" But the truth of it is, when we break down your general appreciation of your business into specifics, it may be a very different tale indeed.

WHAT DOES YOUR APPRECIATION METER READ?

To start, take the following quiz. Circle the term that most accurately reflects where you stand relative to each of the following statements:

1) I pause for a moment as I walk in the door and think how fortunate I am to be in this business:

Always   Frequently   Sometimes
Once in a while   Never

2) It's all a blur until I hit my inbox:

Always   Frequently   Sometimes
Once in a while   Never

3) I greet my secretary by name, and ask her how things are going before I take my messages:

Always   Frequently   Sometimes
Once in a while   Never

4) I grab the pile of messages off my secretary's desk on my way in. I don't know if she's there or not.

Always   Frequently   Sometimes
Once in a while   Never

5) I listen attentively to my VP of sales as he reports to me:

Always   Frequently   Sometimes
Once in a while   Never

6) I'm answering the phone and reading email as my VP of sales drones on:

Always   Frequently   Sometimes
Once in a while   Never

7) I leave my office and walk the floors at least once a day to see what's going on and touch base with my employees:

Always   Frequently   Sometimes
Once in a while   Never

8) I'm in my office solid for 8 - 10 hours and I'm out of there. If you want to see me, you gotta come to me.

Always   Frequently   Sometimes
Once in a while   Never

9) I relish the challenge of solving problems for my customers, of proving our excellence at every opportunity:

Always   Frequently   Sometimes
Once in a while   Never

10) Customers are a royal pain in the neck. I deal with them because I have to:

Always   Frequently   Sometimes
Once in a while   Never

If you answered "Always" or "Frequently" to questions 1, 3, 5, 7 and 9, and "Once in a while" or "Never" to questions 2, 4, 6, 8, 10 your appreciation rating is high. Congratulations! Your business will prosper even more from this book.

If you answered "Sometimes" or "Once in a while" to questions 1,3,5,7 and 9, and "Sometimes" or "Once in a while" to questions 2, 4, 6, 8, 10 your appreciation rating is moderate. You have some idea of how appreciation works in business.

If you answered "Never" or "Once in a while" to questions 1, 3, 5, 7 and 9, and "Always" or "Frequently" to questions 2, 4, 6, 8, 10 your appreciation rating is low. You can benefit a great deal from learning how appreciation can be applied in business settings.

Having determined where you are on the Appreciation Meter, here are some ways you can boost your rating, and gain the many performance, productivity and profitability advantages appreciation can bring to your business.

SHIFT YOUR FOCUS

Appreciation is an obsession with value. It is an active, purposeful search for the value or worth of whatever or whomever you come in contact with. Most of the time, your focus as you walk through the doors of your business is on everything that's going wrong: all the problems that you must deal with and somehow solve, or properly delegate to be solved. In the process, you ignore, and most emphatically fail to value, everything that's going right. That's the equivalent of vibrational suicide.

Look at your business with new eyes. Take yourself on an appreciative walk-through of your day. Deliberately search for what you could appreciate and could find of value in every moment of that day.

> "I was appalled when I took my 'Appreciation walk.' I thought I was a very positive and appreciative person, but apparently, I'm not! I own a large physical therapy outfit here in town The first thing I see when I walk in are all the things that are out of whack, like the fluorescents that are still flickering, or the towels that haven't been picked up.
>
> "I had to really stop myself to notice what I value--like

how spacious and comfortable our reception area is, or that the towel service is almost always prompt. But when my manager tells me my top therapist is out sick, I immediately find myself irritated and angry, instead of appreciating the therapists who are in today, and valuing how they and my front office people will handle the re-bookings of that therapist's clients. And this is just the first 10 minutes of my day!"
John R., owner

Help yourself shift your focus by asking your managers and department heads to regularly report what's working, where the greatest progress is being made, who's going the extra mile, anything and everything that is of value in their department. Take a few moments to acknowledge and appreciate with your reporting manager, asking for more details, being enthusiastic about what they have to say, cheering the report so that your appreciation vibration is strong, clear and well focused.

PROBLEM SOLVING WITH APPRECIATION

When a problem inevitably comes up, refer first to your appreciation reports and find something you can value with which to springboard your problem solving.

"I feel like I'm re-wiring my brain to think differently. Now, when a problem comes up, say in maintenance, instead of picking up the phone and yelling at the head of maintenance, I go to my weekly appreciation reports and find something useful there. Then I pick up the phone and tell the head of maintenance that the cleaning crew is doing a much better job since he spoke to them, and the trainers have mentioned that the workout rooms are more pleasant to work in now.

"Then, for example, instead of saying 'Fix the fluorescent lights already, would ya? They're driving everybody buggy,' I say 'We're still having problems with the fluorescent lights. Do you have any ideas on what to do there?' and wait to see what he will say.

"More often than not, he'll come up with a good solution and be willing to implement it. Then all I have to do is acknowledge how good his idea is, thank him profusely, let him know how much I value his contribution to the success of our facility, and I'm off to the next problem."
Rob M., workout facility manager

By asking employees what they think might resolve a problem, you are actively demonstrating how you value their abilities. When valued this way, most workers will try to think of good solutions. Many may even come up with better solutions than you would have thought of for the simple reason that they often know the workings of their particular job or department better than anyone. If employees don't come up with a solution right away, you can always ask them to brainstorm or think about it and get back to you. By doing so, you are acknowledging their value before usurping it with yours.

This is, of course, not to say that everyone else will solve problems for you, but that in valuing your workers' ability to do so, you vibrationally increase the chances that they will. In the meantime, by continuing to acknowledge their value, you increase the possibility that they will become proactive and regularly and eagerly seek solutions to future problems.

When you see value in people, you free them up to be more creative, more innovative and more valuable to your business. In addition, when workers are part of the decision-making or the creation of a solution, they own it and are therefore more willing to do what it takes to see it through.

APPRECIATION INCREASES YOUR MENTAL EFFECTIVENESS

Appreciation puts you in the proper mental and physical state to make you a better executive, supervisor or manager. Simply put, when your heart and brain work better, you not only enjoy better health and well-being, you are more effective on the job.

> "My job as CEO of an international paper company means I'm faced with a mountain of problems from every quarter. From production through sales, I have to make decisions on all levels--local, national, international. I also have an agonizing sense of responsibility and accountability to our shareholders. I've learned how valuable it is to take a moment to appreciate--even in the midst of a crisis.
>
> "I appreciate the overall health of our company, the continuing validity of our product, the solid staff I have all over the world. I really think about how much I value all that and am truly grateful for it. Once I appreciate, I feel better. I'm calmer, more focused and more energized. I'm better able to face the latest challenge. Because it seems to help me think more clearly, I often take 'appreciation moments' throughout my day--especially when I'm most stressed."
> Margaret T., CEO

This CEO's experience reflects what we know from science: focusing on sincere thoughts and feelings of appreciation not only eases your heart rate into a harmonious pattern, but brings your nervous system into balance and greatly diminishes your stress response. All of your bodily systems work in greater harmony, bringing not only immediate relief, but also long-term benefits since the harmful effects of stress are greatly lessened. The CEO's experience of "thinking more clearly" likewise reflects what we know happens to the brain when you are in a state of active appreciation: greater clarity and focus, better motivation, enhanced memory flexibility of thought.

Taking "appreciation moments" throughout your day will help you maintain the physical and mental well-being you need to be an effective, powerful CEO, manager or department head.

BE SINCERE

For appreciation to be effective, it must be sincere. You cannot simply mouth words of valuing or gratitude and be done with it. Appreciation is a vibration, and vibration responds to underlying intention, not to words. If your intention is to express how much you value an employee's contribution to a project, you could simply say "Oh, my" and your vibration of valuing would align with a vibration of value within the employee. This leads to a valued state of being.

If, on the other hand, you discourse for 15 minutes on how you value the person's contribution yet mean not a word, your vibration would be one of manipulation, not appreciation. You would align with--you guessed it--a vibration of manipulation within the employee. The employee would not feel valued, but somehow conned. The resulting state of being would probably be distrust.

This being said, the power of genuine appreciation is limitless. It is most effective, as we will see in later chapters, when you value specific aspects of a worker's behavior, rather than offering a general "You're great" pat on the back.

ACKNOWLEDGE PEOPLE

Your impact as head of a company or head of your department cannot be overestimated. How you greet and acknowledge the people you interact with on a daily basis is of great vibrational import. When you fail to greet employees, vendors or co-workers in an appreciative manner, they feel as if they do not exist for you. This aligns with a vibration of "I don't matter." People who feel they don't matter to you are highly unlikely to respond with valued behaviors.

Make people feel valued and valuable by looking them in the eye when talking. It shows you are really focusing on the human being standing before you, and if only for an instant, appreciating that person's existence on this earth. Allow a smile or pleasant expression to grace your face when you say "Hi" or "How ya doin'?" even if your contact is fleeting. You may think this is too much effort or takes too much time, but in reality, it's just a habit to acquire, and doesn't take more than a nano-second.

If possible, use a person's name when you greet them. Using a person's name is not simply a matter of politeness. Names are a symbol of our identity, of our being. Your name is , to you, the most important word in any language, and you will respond to your name more acutely than to any other word. By using a person's name, you are acknowledging their importance and value, and are reinforcing your vibration of appreciation for their very existence.

Being noticed in such a valuing and appreciative manner by you as the head of the company or department matters hugely to those who work for and with you-- a great deal more than you probably realize.

> "What's nice is our boss--the big boss--he's not so above us he can't say 'hi.' I'm always tickled that he remembers my name. I mean he hardly gets to our department more than a couple of times a year. We're a very big company. But he always looks me in the eye and says 'Hi, Mary!' and I get the feeling he really sees me, you know? Makes me proud of working for the company."
> Mary C., office clerk

The Power of Appreciation in Business

It doesn't matter where on the pay scale a person is, from the cleaning crew to the CFO, acknowledging others in a valuing way entrains value from them.

> "I'm in and out of the CEO's office 10 times a day as VP of Marketing. Every time, he actually looks at me and smiles or says something before we begin discussing the matter at hand. I've worked for other CEO's and half the time I've felt like any old marketing person would do. With this guy, I feel like who I am matters, and I'll tell you--I work twice as hard because of it."
> Vera G., VP of Marketing

The CEO of several catalog companies (Professional Cutlery Direct, LLC, Cooking Enthusiast and Uno Alla Volta, LLC), Terri Alpert, has built her business to a sales volume of $14 million in 11 years. Her manager, customer relations, Joe Angelicola, says, "I can tell you that top to bottom everyone is appreciated. Everyone is known by name. Our CEO will walk around tomorrow [December 22] to shake the hand of everyone here, to tell them thank you, and give them a gift. Knowing Terri's business acumen, she believes it is very, very important to thank employees."

WATCH YOUR TALK

If you want to know what you truly think and feel about your business, listen to how you communicate with employees, vendors and others. Listen also to the words you use in talking about your product or service. If you want others to value your business, product or service, then you must value it.

Here are but a few of the ways you can either appreciate or depreciate your business with the words you choose:

Do you say "the company," "the business," "the product" or do you say "our company," "our business," "our product"?"Our" implies more than ownership, it implies pride of ownership--value. Saying "our" invites others to participate in that value with you.

Do you refer to the first day of the workweek as "awful Mondays," respond to difficulties with "Oh, great, another problem," or refer to work as "Another day, another dollar," in a regular manner? These and similar expressions do not speak to valuing your business. Pay attention to the phrases you use repeatedly. These point to a frame of mind that in turn points to your vibration around the subject.

How do you refer to customers, vendors and employees? Are these terms value-enhancing or value diminishing? Remember, as the manager, department head or executive, your vibration is the most important vibration relative to those you work with. Whatever thoughts and feelings you are expressing through your habitual use of language are the thoughts and feelings others will align with vibrationally.

Words are both expressions of thought and shapers of thought. If the words you use point to a less than appreciative vibration, you can help shape that vibration by changing the words you choose. Bear in mind, however, that you must be sincere about the change. Vibration cannot be fooled.

How often do you say "thank you" or other expressions such as "Appreciate it," "I appreciate that," "Thanks so much"? It's almost impossible to overdo such expressions as long as they are sincere.

"Watch your talk" isn't just about verbal statements you make about your people, product and customers. It's also about the non-verbal statements you make through the physical condition and layout of your company or department.

Look around your business. What do the working conditions say about how you value, or fail to value, those who work for and with you? What is the condition of the work environment? The restrooms? Lunch areas? Do you offer daycare or other amenities such as a workout facility? How about the equipment? Machinery? Supplies? Tools? What needs fixing? Could employees benefit from better lighting? Would a new coat of paint make a dreary work area brighter? How about your reception area? What does it say to your customers and visitors? Is your parking lot great for the higher-ups but lousy for everybody else? What about security? The list goes on and on.

Watch your non-verbal talk by assessing how working conditions reflect your valuing of your employees, product and customers. Make changes that will demonstrate and further your genuine appreciation for all. By using ingenuity and creativity, many positive changes can be made with only a small amount of effort and expense.

WALK YOUR TALK

Appreciation is not a concept. Appreciation is a way of thinking and feeling that must be expressed in action. Valuing people and your product or service must be demonstrated physically. The first and easiest way to do this is to catch workers in the act of doing something valuable, something "right."

> Barkley Evergreen & Partners Public Relations has developed an entire program, the "Whodunit Award," designed solely to catch employees in the act of doing something "right," something extraordinary. The

company, recognized as one of the top firms in the country by leading trade media including PRWeek and The Holmes Report, is one of seven operating companies at Barkley Evergreen & Partners, Inc. the largest employee-owned firm of its kind in the U.S.

"Whodunit" is a recognition program structured after the popular board game "Clue." It involves "witnesses" who catch a "perpetrator" (the nominee) in the act of doing something "extraordinary" which represents the characteristics of Barkley Evergreen's "soul," that is to say something "passionate, innovative, smart/savvy, respected, ethical and experienced." "Supporting testimony" is requested from "the victim, witnesses or accomplices." The value of the program is undeniable. The company has maintained a 90% employee retention rate, and as Lori Hardy, Account Supervisor, states, "Our employees are motivated to do incredible things to win the award."

So often, we are steadfastly focused on catching employees doing something wrong. In truth, catching people doing something right, something of value, is far more beneficial to your business.

Make a habit of walking around the business on a spontaneous and unanticipated basis. Using the appreciation reports gleaned from your department heads, let workers know that you appreciate a specific aspect of their valued effort. Tell them how their "good act" was noticed and what it means to you or to the company.

Know enough about what workers are doing in different departments so you can make meaningful comments about their contributions. Specific comments are much more appreciated than general ones. Saying "you're doing a great job" isn't as personally meaningful to an employee as "the specs you wrote up on Project X really made a difference to our customer," or "Noticing that bug in our system software and bringing it to IT's attention was a big help in getting our new product out on schedule."

Ask employees what they're working on right now. Engage them in conversation about it, even if only for a minute. Wanting to know their thoughts lets employees know that what they think and what they have to say is valuable. Always remember to look workers in the eye, use their name and be genuinely interested in their comments.

By walking through the departments in this manner, you are sending a powerful vibration that affirms the importance of the individual department members to the business. Important enough that you, an obviously busy person, value your employees sufficiently to rub elbows with them, if only for a brief moment.

LEAD BY EXAMPLE

As you express yourself differently to and about those involved with your business and demonstrate your valuing of people directly, vibrations of others will match up with yours. The more intense and passionate your appreciation, the stronger your vibration and the more easily others will be entrained by you.

> "At first it was weird having our CEO come down and spend time with the crews. It seemed awkward, frankly. But he seemed so sincere about it, when he'd thank a crewmember or comment on some work a team had completed, that we kind of all relaxed and started looking forward to his visits. Once he casually handed me a cup of coffee and said 'Cream or sugar?' I nearly fell over. I started telling him some of what's really going on down here and he listened. I mean he really paid attention and things changed. I never had that happen before."
> Gerald D., mechanic

A frequently unanticipated but most valuable consequence of valuing those who work with and for you in this direct way is that you'll get value right back. The crew leader shared information with the CEO that the CEO would otherwise have only learned when things started going seriously wrong. This is a typical consequence of what happens when you appreciate. When workers feel your genuine valuing of them, they value you in return. Your business thrives in such an atmosphere of mutual respect and appreciation.

Southwest Airlines, now 34 years in business, with 31,000 employees, has the unique distinction of being the only airline after 9/11 that continued to make money. Southwest not only has a culture of appreciation, but specifically looks for individuals who are appreciative, who have an attitude of valuing others.

> Per Melanie Jones, Programs Manager, Public Relations Department, and Sunny Stone, Director of Culture Activities at Southwest; "People who are chosen to be leaders at Southwest have it already. We hire for attitude and train for skill. If you have the attitude but not the skill, you'll get the job over someone who thinks they are wonderful."

Some people may fall out of the mix. An individual completely without a vibration of appreciation cannot be entrained. Whether it is an employee, vendor or customer, that person may not, in the grand scheme of things, be a good "fit" for your business. After all, if they cannot value your products or services, how valuable can they be to your company?

LIVE UP TO YOUR PROMISES

Whether you are in the business of producing products or providing services--or both, making sure that your product/service lives up to its promises is a major component of the appreciative paradigm. You must value your product/service with such intensity and focus that you would never allow your product/service to fulfill less than its promise. Only then can you ask others--your employees, managers and customers--to value your product/service. It is your responsibility to give substance, reality, to that promise.

Richard Van Doren, Vice President of marketing for See's Candies, Inc., a California based eighty-four year old company founded in 1921 with 5,800 employees, and a sales volume of $300,000,000, says: "I was thinking last night about why our employees have such long tenures here and I think it comes down to our integrity. Charles See started the company using [his mother] Mary's recipes. Mary said, "Don't you ever compromise my recipes or you're finished." So, Charles set the foundation, and that's been continued ever since.

"During the depression, when there was rationing of food, Charles See wouldn't compromise on the quality of the ingredients. He would make the candy he could, and when it was gone, he would close up shop and say 'That's all we have today, come back tomorrow.' Integrity is very important to us. Our motto is 'Quality without compromise.'

"For instance, when it comes to our ingredients, whatever the FDA standards are, we strive to do better every time. And we search for a supplier until we find one who will work with us to achieve that quality. Most of our ingredients are purchased in California, except for our ginger from Australia and our pecans from Georgia. We've been with Challenge butter since 1923 and we have a good relationship with them. Our product is such high quality and our employees realize the amount of money we spend on our product. I think it makes them feel good about the company."

People work best when they believe that their work has meaning, and a large part of that meaning is derived from the meaningfulness ascribed to the product. Regardless of the industry, people's conviction that their product/service is the best is what motivates them to do their best. They feel a part of something worthwhile, and that justifies their effort. A vibration of worthiness entrains worthiness.

"I work for a company that makes wooden brackets, closet rods, that kind of thing. And you'd think well, a bracket is a bracket. But our CEO founded the company and he's absolutely dedicated to us making the very best brackets. Which is pretty much what any company will tell you.--I've worked in different parts of this business and everybody says 'We want to make the best.' But with this company, it's different. It goes all out to make sure ours are the sturdiest brackets, nicely designed and all that.

"What really impressed me, is how our CEO will tell you about what it means to a family to have good brackets in their home; how our brackets hold up the shelves kids put their baseball trophies on; how our closet rods make mom's jobs easier because hangers slide easy on ours, and on and on. Well those images stick in my head. I take pride in my job, because of how much what we do, when we do it right, matters to people."
Theo F., lathe operator

CREATE A CULTURE OF APPRECIATION

Collect stories of work done well, of those who went the extra mile and of bright spirits in the face of daunting problems. Make heroes of the ordinary men and women who work for and with you.

We are starved for recognition, for genuine applauding of our talents and skills. We long for and want to be heroes--those who prevail against all odds, those who win. The enormous success of TV reality shows is largely predicated on our need to be valued and to be seen as valuable. We want to be appreciated for who we are and want the opportunities to be winners.

Celebrate the value of whoever within your company deserves it, regardless of position or department. Everyone, from VPs to data entry workers, longs for appreciation. Celebrate workers' "good acts" outside of work as well. Foster a general climate of valuing people and both the surrounding community and your company will reap the benefits.

Using your weekly department appreciation reports, create a weekly "one-sheet" of what has been valued and appreciated in every department. Let it be purely devoted to good acts. Post the one-sheet prominently in every department. Encourage its reading at your weekly staff meetings. Make sure good acts by vendors, cleaning crews, and other ancillary workers are included in the and see that the one-sheet is distributed to them as well.

Discourage negative talk and gossip about anyone or anything. Don't indulge in "the economy is terrible" talk, or "stockholders are a nuisance" or "committee meetings, what a waste of time" type conversations. Don't diminish the power of your appreciation vibration by trashing or bashing others.

Address problems as solutions-in-the-making, and spend as little time as possible finding fault. Seek always to educate yourself and others as to how to make things better, rather than wasting time and vibration on pinning blame.

FOLLOW THROUGH

Appreciation is not a fad; it is not a technique. It is a paradigm shift, a new approach. If you want to see the tremendous advantage an appreciative approach can make to your business, you must consistently infuse your business with appreciative thoughts and practices. You must personally encourage, support, and lead the way.

It all starts with you. From you, appreciation can spread throughout every layer of your company and its business.

CHAPTER 3

EMPLOYEES:
THE GREAT DIVIDE

APPRECIATION AND JOB RETENTION

United States Department of Labor data shows that the *number one* reason people leave their jobs is that *they do not feel appreciated.*

With this recent statistic ("How Full is Your Bucket?" Rath, T. & Clifton, D. p.31), there is no longer any doubt that appreciation is vital to employee retention and high performance and productivity levels. Appreciation can no longer be dismissed as "just another HR fad." Valuing employees is more than handing them a paycheck each week. Appreciation can't be reserved "for customers only." As important as customers are, without workers to provide your product or service competently and efficiently, your business will fail.

The Power of Appreciation in Business

Contrary to popular wisdom, money isn't a sufficient motivator to keep employees on the job or doing good work. If it were, people would cite "lack of adequate compensation" as the primary reason for leaving jobs. They don't. Although a certain level of monetary compensation is essential to hire and retain good employees, money is what scientists call a "necessary but not sufficient condition." It's good, but it's not enough. From the warehouse worker to the CFO, dollars will not keep that employee coming in day after day with the enthusiasm and desire to do the best job possible. For that, you need appreciation.

Do your current appreciation efforts satisfy your employees' appreciation needs? Formal recognition, such as rewards banquets for top producers or employee-of-the-month awards, is a step in the right direction, but these programs don't address the needs of enough of your employees, nor do such programs necessarily represent an obsession with value.

Ray Pelletier, professional speaker, author ("It's All About Service"), consultant and CEO of The Pelletier Group, conducted an extensive study of morale in the U.S. Air Force. Despite the fact that the Air Force is very good about recognizing accomplishments, Pelletier says, "what they [the men and women in uniform] were screaming for was appreciation. Appreciation would be a driving factor as to why they should re-enlist. In every group studied, it was about appreciation, not recognition."

Recognition and gratitude, as wonderful as they are, aren't enough. Speaking to the value of all employees in a multitude of ways is the first and most critical component of your appreciation efforts.

FROM HIGH HOPES TO BARE MINIMUM

Studies show that the majority of employees enter a new job with high hopes, eagerness and a desire to do their best. Only a very small percent are what might be considered hostile or toxic employees who should never have been hired in the first place. Typically, somewhere during the first four to six months the eagerness and desire of most employees wane. The job becomes "just a job." "I have to go to work" replaces "I want to go to work," and employees do just what is required of them, if that.

There are of course, the exceptions, those few self-motivated individuals who do their best no matter what. Unfortunately, the majority become relatively indifferent and lethargic employees--that large bell shape in the middle of the normal curve is what will drag down your business.

The Power of Appreciation in Business

At this point, the Great Divide sets in. Employees do as little as possible--just enough to keep their jobs and satisfy their conscience that they are earning their paychecks. They have no desire to go the extra mile or come up with innovative ways of increasing company productivity or profitability.

Said in the language of expectations, your employees are willing and expecting to do the bare minimum.

You, meanwhile, and your managers expect great things from these same employees. You expect them to come in early (or at least on time), and to leave not a second before quitting time. You expect your employees to be rarely, if ever, late or absent. You expect your employees to work with zeal and passion at their appointed tasks-- going the extra mile when needed. More than that, you harbor secret hopes that your employees will step up even when not called upon and will develop great, business-improving ideas on their own.

The problem is, that despite your high expectations of your employees, you are not treating them in accord with those expectations. Therefore, your expectations have no power. Your expectations, regardless of how passionately felt, cannot on their own entrain the behavior you hope for. Your employees are essentially giving according to what they are receiving (like attracts like). In the absence of appreciation, they see themselves only working for a paycheck--that necessary but not sufficient condition.

Employees: the Great Divide

Your and your employees' expectations, at this point, are on opposite sides of the Great Divide.

Enter appreciation. Appreciation is how you bridge the Great Divide and synchronize your employees' expectations to your own.

Employees need to feel appreciated on two fronts. They need to know:
- what they *do* is valuable and

- who they *are* is valuable.

Appreciation is more than a technique; it is a paradigm shift. How you show your employees the value of what they do and who they are involves much more than the traditional approach of "This Quarter's Top Producer" or year-end bonuses.

APPRECIATE YOUR EMPLOYEES' WORK

One of the most important functions of work is that it brings a sense of purpose to people's lives. We need to feel that what we do is meaningful and that it has value. Employees' initial passion for the job peters out as they fail to see how what they do matters. They begin to feel like interchangeable parts, pieces of a machine that can do just as well with or without them.

Here are some ways to let employees know that what they do does matter and you value their contribution.

The baseline: communicate employees' duties and responsibilities clearly so they know what is expected of them. You can't live up to what you don't know.

> "I was really excited when I started my new job. I'd been a VP of Marketing for a number of years with another company, but this was a bigger company with a bigger salary. It was a great career move for me. I wanted to do my best. I was given a group of accounts, an office and a budget--and that was pretty much it. I knew the basics, of course, and I tried to figure out what to do from the few scribbled notes my predecessor had left, but I was insecure about how the company wanted specific accounts handled. I ended up having to ask my boss all sorts of tedious picky questions, what she thought of a given approach. She pretty much just said 'That sounds fine – go for it.'
>
> "Well I did, but I never felt confident about my choices. I mean, she was always in a rush, and half the time I'm not sure she even heard me. So when I got my

Employees: the Great Divide

first review and it said 'adequate,' I was devastated! I wanted so badly to do really well, but how could I when I never really knew what I was supposed to do? Even when I asked why I received an 'adequate' and what could I do to improve, I never got much guidance, just a, 'You'll improve over time,' which was meaningless. Improve what? How?

"The pizzazz kind of went out of the job for me after that. I do my job OK, but I put a lot more time and attention elsewhere. I mean the company just doesn't seem that important to me any more."
Rene G., VP of Marketing

Don't assume employees know what you expect. New employees may have held similar jobs elsewhere, but each company and its job expectations are different. Failing to give your employee proper guidance is a demonstration of indifference. It's as if you were saying, "I can't be bothered helping you out. You're just another body. If you figure it out, fine, if you don't, I can always hire someone else." How devaluing!

Van Doren, of See's Candies, says: "We treat the employees like we treat the product. Quality without compromise. We train our employees so they know what we want. We give them a sense of history. They know they are part of something bigger. We use 30 of Mary See's recipes. And nothing changes. I think it is like a comfort zone for people. You can only buy See's candy at See's stores. You can buy See's gift certificates at Costco now, but you still have to come into the store to get the candy. And our stores are still the same black and white, same uniforms, same service, same candy. When you come in for your favorite piece of candy, it will taste exactly the way you remember it.

"In fact, if we can't get the ingredients that meet our standards for a particular candy, we will not make that type until we can. We have sons, daughters, cousins, moms, dads, etc., working for us, all from the same family. I gave service awards out recently for a cousin and two sisters from the same family. They were getting 30-year service awards! It's magic. And hard to explain. I guess it comes down to that integrity. "Quality without compromise," [is what] we also apply to our employees."

Jones, of Southwest Airlines, says; "We also encourage our Employees to be themselves and to treat others the way you want to be treated. We teach them to treat each other with respect and kindness. You don't hear the phrase 'that's not my job' around here. If someone asks for help from a peer, they'll bend over backward to help because of how they are treated by that person."

SHOW VALUE BY ASKING QUESTIONS

One of the least used yet most effective means to acknowledge the value of employees is by asking them questions. A good method to determine whether employees have been given sufficient instruction to accomplish their tasks is to ask how they see their job duties and responsibilities.

> "One thing I like about my job is I'm never in the dark about what I'm supposed to do. We're a big company and they change things from time to time. Well, my supervisor has this checklist system. Every time there's a policy change, or a change in how we're supposed to do things, he sends round an updated checklist of our duties.
>
> "Then he holds a meeting and goes over it with us, mostly asking us, 'OK, guys, tell me how this changes what you do,' which really helps, because half the time I'm thinking the change means one thing, and another of us thinks it means something else. It takes a bit of discussion before we all are on the same page.

My supervisor always does this with real good humor. He never makes you feel stupid or on the spot."
Pete H., biochemical lab researcher

This group of employees and their supervisor's expectations are always well synchronized. When you value your employees, you set them up for success. Letting people know clearly what is expected of them demonstrates your belief that what they do is important, that it matters.

"You wouldn't think the file clerks would get much attention in an office of this size. We have well over 200 CPAs here. But when a new file clerk is hired, first thing that happens is our manager drags the newbie over to this big chart on the wall. It has pictures and drawings that show what happens to a filed document and how important proper filing is to the overall success and reputation of our firm. You don't feel like you're just some lowly file clerk at the very bottom of the work food chain. You feel like what you do matters.

"It makes you take pride in your work. I know if I misfile something, all heck breaks loose. But more importantly, when I file correctly, I know exactly how I'm responsible for a client's welfare, and that feels good. Our manager reminds us of it constantly, we even have a 'most correctly filed files' award every week!"

Jean P., file clerk

TELL EMPLOYEES HOW THEIR WORK MATTERS

It's hard to feel that your work matters if you don't know how or why. Let employees know how their job fits with the overall goals and purpose of the company. Right from the get-go, let employees know how important their contribution will be to the overall company.

> "We manufacture medical products so we employ everyone from assembly line workers to delivery and sales people. I'm part of the team that maintains the assembly line equipment. When I first got here, the crew chief spent a whole day taking me around the plant, the offices--the works. He explained to me what everybody's job was and how it all fit with the company's purpose and attitude: 'Do it right, save a life.'
>
> "I got the big picture in my head right off, and I know I'm a part of all that. It feels good to know my team matters, and that everybody knows it. What we do

isn't taken for granted. It makes me proud to work for the company."
Ronald B., maintenance engineer

GIVE APPRECIATIVE FEEDBACK

Give frequent, specific and targeted feedback on work done right. Point out the value of what the employee has accomplished and how the employee's effort contributes to the excellence of the product and the success of the business.

Far too often, the only time employees know what their value to the company is, is when they don't have any; the employee has done something wrong, or incorrectly. Psychology has long proven that people respond far better to positive feedback than to negative. When you consistently let your employees know what they are doing right, you accomplish several goals:

- you keep employees on the right track since they are likely to repeat behaviors they have been praised for,

- by valuing their efforts, you increase employees'

sense of competence, which in turn, leads to increased competence on the job,

- when letting employees know how their good acts further the excellence and success of your product or service, you reinforce their pride in contributing to that success.

The key to successful appreciative feedback is that it must be immediate as well as specific and sincere. It's not something to be put on your monthly calendar as "Say something nice to John today." Instead, whenever a piece of work is properly done or a valiant effort is made, appreciation should be forthcoming. The more immediate the feedback, the greater its impact.

Giving immediate feedback makes it easier for the feedback to be specific. You can target your appreciation more effectively when the event is fresh in your mind. For example, "Thanks for getting that shipment to Des Moines ready and loaded in time for today's pick-up. I know it took a lot of focus and a lot of extra phone calls" is more valuing and therefore more effective than "You're doing a good job," said two weeks after the fact and prompted by nothing in particular other than remembering "Oh, yeah, I need to appreciate my employees."

You're more likely to be genuine and to be heard as genuine when your appreciative comments are immediate and specific. "You're doing a good job" may be sincere and may be heard as such the first few times, but after awhile, such expressions feel too generic and automatic to mean much of anything.

Immediate feedback enhances your employees' willingness and ability to synchronize with what you expect of them.

> "I always know where I'm at with my boss. I'll get an email saying 'good second draft, especially the re-wording on point 5b,' or 'your inclusion of subparagraph H hit home.' I like that she pays attention to that kind of stuff. Of course, I put effort into my work because I want to do things well, but it sure keeps my motivation high when I know she's paying attention and appreciates what I'm doing."
> Marie G., paralegal

ADDRESS POOR PERFORMANCE APPRECIATIVELY

Of course, employees don't always perform well. Poor performance or productivity must be addressed. However, a "This work is terrible, do it again," or "Can't you do anything right?"

devalues the employee who will respond with an equally devalued response (like attracts like), such as "It's not my fault," or a variety of sullen, indifferent (the famous "whatever"), defensive, or upset reactions. None of these contribute to the future success of your product or service.

Think about the employee's value, whatever you can genuinely and legitimately value, and start with that: "You've been showing a lot of progress lately. I really appreciate the effort you've been making, especially in learning the new software." Only then do you address the area that's not working. For example, "Now, let's take a look at your time management. It's not where it needs to be yet. Tell me what that's about for you."

When you start by appreciating and valuing what employees are doing right, they are much more able to listen appreciatively to your corrections and act on them. Like attracts like, vibration matches up with like vibration.

GET EMPLOYEES INVOLVED

Employees are not mindless robots (much as employers might wish they were given the imagined convenience). It is far easier to synchronize employee expectations when you involve your employees in the decisions affecting their work. Ask questions;

actively solicit better ways of doing things. Asking employees their opinions is a powerful way to let them know you value how they do their job.

> "The higher-ups had decided to implement a new engineering software system. I'm one of the five electrical engineers in our department so the change was going to be huge for me. We'd been working comfortably with the old software for years and there was a lot of grumbling about the change.
>
> "Our supervisor sat down with us. Instead of just announcing, 'Here's the new software package, deal with it,' he asked, 'OK, what are you going to need to make this new software work for you?' That started us thinking in a completely different way. We were able to talk about our worries about getting behind on our current projects during the change over; what the learning curve was going be; how much training we'd be getting.
>
> "We actually worked out a plan together for each of us to learn a different aspect of the program, depending on our specialties and then teach it to the others. It worked out really well--oh, there were some kinks to iron out and bumps along the way, but the transition

Employees: the Great Divide

was amazingly smooth. I think we all committed to the change in a more positive way than if it had just been imposed on us."
Matt R., electrical engineer

Not only did the supervisor demonstrate his valuing of his engineers by asking their opinion, he used those opinions to create an efficient change process.

USE EMPLOYEE IDEAS

Listen to and use your employees' ideas. Few things make employees feel more valued than being listened to and having their ideas implemented.

Southwest Airlines is a great believer in listening to Employee ideas. Programs Manager Jones says: "Many of the innovations for which Southwest has become known, some of which have been critical to our success, came from Employees in the rank and file. For example, in the early days, Southwest had four 737 airplanes to fly a four airplane schedule. Southwest was struggling financially, and we didn't have the money to make payroll, so we had to sell one of those aircraft for cash.

"An Employee proposed that it would be possible to operate the four-plane schedule with just three aircraft if the planes were turned quickly on the ground and if the ground crew expedited its their duties. This would require, at that time, an unheard of ground time for Southwest aircraft--from the time the plane pulled into the gate to unload passengers and baggage and then loaded up again and pushed away from the gate--of 10 minutes.

"This particular innovation has been a critical factor in our success, and while the ground time has crept up during recent years because of heavier passenger loads, security requirements, etc., Southwest still has an incredibly low ground time--one that is respected and unmatched in the industry. It is just one piece in our success formula--after all, the planes are making money only when they are in the air.

"More recently, another Employee, in his own time, played around with a program that would schedule our aircraft more efficiently, optimizing their usage. This program has been enhanced and put in place, and now our entire fleet is flying on this "optimized schedule" giving us what amounts to more aircraft usage within the schedule to add more flights with the same number of planes. The optimized schedule is expected to bring Southwest tens of millions of dollars of added revenue."

It goes without saying that each employee's contribution must be acknowledged and praised. Having your ideas implemented feels great but no one knowing it was your idea feels awful.

"Our team works on a project basis. We all have our different functions on any given project. Before the reorganization, our team leader--our manager really-- would come in, tell us what the project was and what he expected from each of us. He'd send us on our way and we'd each do our thing. We'd meet once a week, every week. He'd check on our progress, make suggestions and off we'd go again. But after the reorganization, everything changed. I mean-- changed!

"Our team leader got us together, told us what the project was--and then asked us how each of us expected to contribute. I was stunned. Nobody said anything for the longest time, then one guy said 'Well, I'm QC, so I guess I'll develop the quality specs.' And then the rest of us chimed in. It started getting downright exciting. After that, our team leader gave us a couple of suggestions and off we went.

"When we met again the next week, our team leader asked us where we were at, checked our progress. It was the same-o, same-o to all the previous weekly meetings, and I started to lose interest. But then he looked right at me, and said 'From your perspective, what can you offer to QC?' I went, 'Huh?' I'm mean, I'm part of the design group; what do I know about QC? He said, 'What do you think would enhance QC? Make it better?' I wanted to say 'I don't know,' but I did know. I just had never been asked before.

"I said my bit, and then he went around the table, getting each of us to talk about our ideas--for each other. It took us a while to get going, but once we did, it was the most exciting meeting I'd ever been to. All of a sudden, the project meant something to all of us. I wanted the whole project to succeed, not just my part.

"Our team leader kept track of whose ideas were used (and how) on this cool whiteboard with colors and flow lines and arrows—it was great. We stuck with this system and I've got to tell you, those projects fly out of our department now. We're proud of them, and

Employees: the Great Divide

of each other."
Anne T., software designer

Listening to employees is a good idea in all areas of your business.

Van Doren, of See's Candies, says: "For the employees, we have contests with good prizes. We've sent people on cruises, like Princess cruises, and trips. Nice prizes. The district managers come up with the ideas. They often ask the employees for fun ideas. We pick one and that becomes the contest. Contests for things like who can sell the most salted nuts. We do fun things with the employees. We have Mary See's face all over. In the plants, we have big cutouts of her and the employees put hairnets on her."

CELEBRATE AT EVERY OPPORTUNITY

Don't let a single opportunity for celebration go unheeded. Achieving goals, finishing a training program, going the extra mile--all deserve valuing and appreciation.

Formal recognition has long been well understood by business: top producers are almost always accorded awards and special status.

What's not been well understood is the importance of awards or symbols to mark a diversity of achievements and effort.

Awards can be simple: applause, a humorous "gold star," or a "congrats!" email or card. Awards can be elaborate: a cruise, a dinner for two, tickets to a cherished ball game and of course, that ever appreciated award – cash.

Reasons for an award can be as varied as receiving a glowing customer thanks, pitching in to help without being asked, mentoring a new hire with graciousness and good humor. There is no need to restrict appreciation to that annual awards banquet where too few receive the company's applause for too few reasons.

> Angelicola, of Professional Cutlery Direct, LLC, etc, says: "When an employee receives a "kudos" letter or phone call from a customer, we send a PCD [Professional Cutlery Direct] email to everyone in the company to let them know. People stop by to congratulate them, give 'em a pat on the back. And I post all those letters right outside my office. I also always call the customer to thank them for the letter or phone call. Also, we have what we call 'PCD Bucks.' When we see someone doing an exceptional job, we give those out and they can be used like cash to purchase from our catalogs. We also might say 'You've done a great job, take the

rest of the day off,' on a Friday afternoon."

Southwest Airlines shows their dedication to Employee suggestions by basing their "Winning Spirit Award" on such suggestions.

Per Jones and Stone; "We have the Winning Spirit Award, which is given every other month by the CEO of our company. An Employee is nominated by his or her peers for an act above and beyond the call of duty. Here are a couple of examples.

"During the recent snowstorms, a military kid flying with us got dropped from the roster and rerouted twice. By the time he got to the second city, he had no money left for an overnight stay in a hotel. The agent at the counter whipped out her own credit card and paid for his hotel that night.

"We had a pilot who finished his shift and was heading home. He has a private plane which he uses to come to work and it was parked at the airport. As he was leaving the terminal, a Customer came up to him, frantic because he had missed the last flight out. The Customer was headed to another city for an organ transplant and he had to be there in the morning to receive it. The pilot flew him in his own plane to his destination city."

An award should show the company's appreciation for something of value to the company, but the award itself should be something of value to the employee.

Many companies go awry on both points. The long established "Employee of the Month" program prevalent in many companies, for example, is highly successful in the first few months when truly exceptional employees are singled out for praise and recognition. After a while, however, the company either rewards the same person repeatedly, causing jealousy and resentment in the ranks, or the company, wishing to avoid such feelings, awards the plaque to a different employee every month.

The company soon strains to find something good about employees whose performance is only adequate and who are chosen primarily because there's no one else left who hasn't been featured. The program loses its value because it isn't rewarding value. To boot, employees are often unsure about how to achieve "Employee of the Month" status. Too often, the award seems predicated on whoever is the supervisor's "pet" at the moment.

This isn't to say the concept isn't good. For example, Southwest Airlines features a "Star of the Month" who is given

Employees: the Great Divide

full-page coverage in its in-flight magazine. The "Star" gets a write-up much like a celebrity. Their opinions are solicited on their job function, they are quoted directly and the article includes comments about the "Star's" family and favorite hobbies. The "Star" gets star photo treatment as well. The magazine article features not a deadpan headshot of the celebrated employee, but a well-composed picture showing the "Star" in a setting representative of their job.

This approach to an "Employee of the Month" program comes much closer to the "catch your employee in the act of doing something valuable" advocated in Chapter 2. The "Star" article tells not only Southwest Employees, but also any Southwest Customer who reads the magazine just how valuable that Employee is to Southwest and why. Such specificity makes it easier for any Employee wanting to be the next "Star" to figure out what qualities and behaviors are prized.

> Barkley Evergreen has found a way around the "Employee of the Month" syndrome by not giving out their "Whodunit" award on a monthly basis, but only when a truly stellar act, with certain definable known characteristics, has been committed by a worthy "perpetrator" and which must be validated by several people. The judging body for the award is composed of two partners plus the last winner of the award, which helps prevent the "supervisor's pet" pattern.

Sometimes you can catch your employee in the act of doing something valuable by creating a competition to foster and support such value. Such, for example, is the case with Ryder System, Inc., a Fortune 500 company providing leading-edge transportation, logistics and supply chain solutions worldwide.

> In addition to their more traditional "top producer" awards, Ryder holds an annual "Top Tech Recognition Program," which recognizes the best among their more than 5,300 technicians, responsible for the safe and productive operation of more than 160,000 vehicles. Technicians are eligible by virtue of being an employee in good standing with no performance problems. From there, the competition gets downright exciting. Technicians go through a variety of written and on-line tests at the local level, and progress to demonstrating their maintenance skills hands-on at the regional level, which leads to the title of "Region Top Tech" for each region.
>
> The Region Top Techs then compete nationally by demonstrating their skills and knowledge hands-on at the highly anticipated, well publicized, final competition. In addition to the various prizes awarded, winners are touted everywhere: in Ryder in-house publications, in local and even national media.

Employees: the Great Divide

Winners are asked for quotes, for their opinions on maintenance, and are lauded by Ryder's higher-ups in the press. For example, Greg Swienton, Ryder's chairman and CEO, is quoted as saying: "These top-performing technicians have surpassed Ryder's stringent operational and safety standards and have proven themselves to be among the nation's best of the best." (Transport Topics, September 6, 2004)

Ryder offers its winners awards increasing in value depending on the status of the winner. In addition to the expected plaques, winners at all levels are given a choice between such options as NASCAR tickets, gift certificates, or "Mac Tools" certificates. Mac Tools certificates give winners the choice of which tools they would like to receive.

Respecting employee award preference is important, because what will be of value to the employee, in terms of an award, will vary from one employee to the next. Some employees thrive on public acknowledgement, others would prefer a quiet "thanks" from their supervisor. Some employees would just love a picture of themselves shaking hands with the "big boss," while others would run from the camera as fast as possible. Some employees think a dinner for two is terrific, others would say, "No thanks, just give me the cash." It's impossible to please everyone with a set award.

Instead, consider having a "Choose your award" sheet that is checked off at the time of hiring and re-visited at year-end review. For example, have a choice of three equally-valuable top awards (depending on the employee level, these will vary widely): dinner for two at a nice restaurant, prime tickets to a local sporting event or a gift certificate to a department store. Include a choice for three equally valuable second tier awards. Of course, you can always have a "No thanks, just give me the cash" box to check.

Including such a sheet at the beginning of the hire is another way to set your employees up for success. You're already assuming they will do well enough to warrant an award. Secondly, it tells new employees that you treat people as individuals, and that you want to value what your employees' value. Regardless of the review the employee receives at year-end, having them revisit this sheet and reassess their choices reaffirms your belief they will do well.

Your belief alone is a vibration that can entrain their belief in their ability to do well – with the consequent good results for the company. As always, for your vibration to successfully entrain your employee's vibration, you must be sincere. You must truly believe in your employee's ability, given effort and diligence, to win those awards.

Employees: the Great Divide

APPRECIATE WHO YOUR EMPLOYEES ARE

Studies have shown that job satisfaction among employees by itself doesn't predict productivity. It is only when job satisfaction is paired with psychological well-being at work that productivity is high. Psychological well-being at work includes a sense of purpose and meaningfulness in one's job, a feeling of accomplishment and of contributing to something worthwhile, recognition of work by superiors, respect of person, fair treatment and a sense of reward commensurate with effort.

Psychological well-being is so important, that if it is low, there will be high turnover, regardless of how satisfied employees are with their job. Valuing your employees' humanity not in the abstract but by how you treat them on the job is the foundation of psychological well-being at work.

Employees who do not feel valued respond with an attitude of "If you don't value me, why should I value you, this job or the customer?" The vibrational alignment is unmistakable. On the other hand, an employee who feels valued by the company experiences increased self-esteem, which in turn, leads to increased competence on the job.

Valuing your employees isn't just so much New Age nice-nice; it directly influences your bottom line.

THE WORKSPACE

Workspaces reflect how you value employees – or don't. Workspaces should be clean, appropriate in design to the job and sufficiently well equipped with whatever employees need to do their job properly.

> "I'm a telemarketer. I don't know why we're treated like the butt-end of the company because without us drumming up the sales, there'd be no company. Anyway, I left my last job because even though I was making good money – we were on commission and I was almost always in the top 10 – the working conditions were awful.
>
> "The place was clean, but the partitions were so thin between our cubicles and our headphones of such poor quality, I always had to jam my hands up against my headphones just to hear myself think, much less hear the customer talk. I'd have to ask customers to repeat things all the time and that's so unprofessional! I was downright embarrassed. Plus, by noon, my nerves were frayed from trying to deal with all the noise. I'd have liked to sit the owner down in my chair

Employees: the Great Divide

and make him do my job for a day and see how he liked it.

"Anyway, they never paid any attention to my complaints. The manager would say 'Oh, we'll get you new headphones' every few months. Well, that never happened. So after a couple of years of it, I quit. And suddenly it's 'Oh, we'll get you those new headphones right away,' and I said, 'Sorry--it's too late. I'm done.' I'd been in telemarketing 10 years, and I just got tired of fighting the same battle at every company. What do they think we are? Animals? Anyway, I'm learning to be a court reporter. At least I won't have to wear broken down headphones."
Joyce C., former telemarketer

Some prospective employees have become very savvy in assessing from the workspace how they are likely to be treated as an employee.

"Restrooms are a dead giveaway as to how you're going to be treated on the job. I don't care what the interviewer tells me about how good people have it at a company; I find a way to check out the employee restroom. And I don't mean the restroom for customers. I look at the one in the back, you know, near the loading dock.

"If that restroom is dirty--paper towels littering the floor, broken toilets or a floor that hasn't been mopped in ages, that tells me two things: management doesn't think much of its workers because that's no way to treat your people and employees don't think much of the company because they aren't making an effort to help keep things clean. No pride. Well, that's enough for me. I'm not working here.

"The nicest employee restroom I ever saw was not only clean, but it had character! Someone had put posters up on the wall, nice tropical scenes, and a thing of funky fake flowers on the sink. There was even some hand lotion. I thought 'OK, these people have some pride in their company and the company values them. I'll work here.'

"The pay wasn't quite as good as another job I was offered, but I signed on anyway. I stayed with that company for eight years until they were bought out and things went downhill. They were great to work for though, until then. We worked hard, but we had a lot of fun."

Rosalie, wholesale produce manager

Employees: the Great Divide

One of the most pitiful recurring scenes in the popular movie "Office Space" was the relocation of an employee to successively dismal working environments, until eventually, he was stuck in the basement with the lights out. As unrealistic as that might seem, it strikes too close to home with too many employees.

DON'T OVERSTRESS GOOD EMPLOYEES

Over stressing your employees by making unreasonable demands on their time and on the effort required to do their job is a failure to value your employees' fundamental humanness. Work with your employees so they feel that the amount of effort they exert on the job is commensurate with their paychecks.

> "I worked for a major health care corporation. I never understood how they were running the place because it seemed like some of us were always overburdened and others were pretty much twiddling their thumbs. I started with a caseload of about 50 patient claim files. It wasn't just numbers crunching. You have to make phone calls, interview patients, decide if an investigation is needed and make decisions that affect people's lives. It was a lot of work, but it was OK. I liked the feeling of helping people.

"Then my co-worker went out on maternity leave and my supervisor asked me if I could handle her caseload. She had about 38, 40 open files. I said, 'it's going to stretch me awfully thin, but all right, I think I can do it for a while.' My supervisor said, 'Let me know if you need help.' I said 'OK.' I began handling these extra cases and staying late on the job to get them done. I was coming in early whenever I could. I was actually proud of the fact that I was managing and I liked helping out.

"Then my supervisor told me my co-worker wasn't coming back after her leave and could I continue handling her cases, seeing what a good job I'm doing until they found someone new? I said, 'OK, but I'm really going to need some help and could they please stop sending new claims to my ex-co-worker's desk?' Because, you see, the claims that were routed to my co-worker's desk kept coming, even though she wasn't there.

"So now I was handling around 80 to 90 cases. I started having bad dreams, my palms were always sweaty and my heart was racing. My husband said I was crazy to be working like that. I asked my supervisor again for help and he said the same thing he always says, 'I've put in a requisition. I'm working on it. Be patient, you're doing a great job.'

"I was trying to be patient, I liked my job, but I was starting to hate coming to work. I got anxious; I lost a lot of weight and was irritable all the time. Then one day, I just snapped. I was finishing up a file; my supervisor walked in, smiled, dropped a whole new load of cases on my desk and walked off, like nothing was happening. I burst into tears. I couldn't stop crying. They had to call the paramedics to take me to the ER. I haven't been able to work since. It's been three months. Every time I think of going back there I want to throw up."
Josie A., claims administrator

A good employee can be broken and rendered ineffectual when not valued as a person, when your only concern is how much work can be produced. It's a lose-lose situation when an otherwise dedicated, valuable employee is lost in this manner.

Stressful periods are inevitable in any business. A company that values its employees understands the cost of that stress to employees and proactively seeks to minimize it.

The catalog business knows a particularly stressful time during the Holidays. The volume of orders increases dramatically, customers place orders with unrealistic time frames, and the usual difficulties encountered with suppliers and delivery services are suddenly multiplied.

> Angelicola, of Professional Cutlery Direct, LLC, etc, talks about how his catalog company helps employees cope with the rush: "Every Wednesday during the holiday season, from right after Thanksgiving up to Christmas, we have a resident chef who prepares lunch for all the employees, both the day and evening crews. That includes the office employees, customer service and the warehouse/distribution employees. At the beginning of December, we brought in a masseuse to give neck massages to any employee who wanted one."

VALUE WHAT IS OF VALUE TO THE EMPLOYEE

You must value what is valuable to the employee. An employee's religion, gender, family, pet, country of origin or hobby, for example, can never be a subjects of derision or scorn. Even jabs under the guise of "I was just kidding" devalue the person. A hit to an employee's self-esteem will reflect itself in their job performance in one way or another.

> "I'm from Morocco. I came over with my family when I was 16. I lived here ever since and became a citizen. It's true, I still have an accent, and I don't always have all the words for things in English like I do in my native tongue. I've often been mistaken for a Muslim or an Iraqi, which upsets me because I'm Christian, like many Moroccans – and Morocco isn't Iraq. After 9/11, I got hate mail stuffed in my mailbox at work and nasty 'cartoons' left at my workstation. It made me very nervous, very worried. At the time, crazy people were killing Pakistanis on the street thinking they were Arabs, and I was afraid I'd be next.
>
> "I took the hate mail and 'cartoons' to my supervisor but he just shoved them aside, and said, 'Ari, you're being too sensitive. It's just someone messing around. Nobody's going to hurt you here.' Easy for him to say. He's as white as they come. It didn't make me feel very good, but I tried to put it out of my head. Then I get transferred to the night shift for no apparent reason. I said, 'Wait a minute, what is this?' and my supervisor said they needed someone on the night shift, and since I don't have kids, I was the most logical choice. I didn't like it, but OK.

"Then I overheard my supervisor talking to another supervisor on the phone, and he said, 'Yeah, I had to move Ari to the nightshift. The day guys didn't want to work next to a Muslim.' My own supervisor! I was shocked. I told him what I'd heard, and that I wasn't a Muslim, I'm a Christian, and besides, what difference does it make what faith you are? We should all be equal in the workplace. You know what he said? 'You shouldn't be eavesdropping, you should be working. Now quit wasting my time and get back to your station.'

"I was outraged. How could he be that way? Twelve years on the job, I was always a good worker, got good reviews and this is how he treats me? Some of the workers started calling me 'Musi.' I told my supervisor. He just laughed and said 'Hey, it's just a nickname. Get over it!' I felt heartsick. How could I keep working hard for a company that cared so little about me? You know, it shouldn't matter what religion you are or what country you are from, nobody deserves to be treated this way. This is America!

"I know my performance has dropped off. I don't enjoy my work like I used to. I get headaches a lot. I

don't feel well much of the time. I just don't care any more. I'm looking for a new job, where I'll be treated like a human being."
Ari H., lab technician

APPRECIATE GRIEVANCES

Give employees opportunities to express concerns and grievances safely and without fear of reprisals. If there's one point that speaks most clearly to how you appreciate your employees, it's how you handle their concerns and grievances. Too often, concerns and grievances are dismissed as unimportant, as some employee "just wanting to make trouble." Indeed, some employees do make trouble, but more often than not, it's because they have not been able to get their concerns or grievances heard.

Studies show that employees' ability to express what's troubling them is critical to their psychological well being on the job. That psychological well being translates into better job performance, less absenteeism, and less turnover – facts a business can ill afford to ignore.

Grievances, especially, are often just dropped into the employee's personnel file and given little more than lip service. These grievances are then held against the employee at time of review, as in "has a behavior problem," or "can't get along well with others." Employees, fearful for their jobs, will often avoid expressing their unhappiness, yet such failure to express grievances is to the detriment of both the employee and the job.

A GENUINE OPEN DOOR POLICY

One way to allow employee grievances to be expressed safely is with an open door policy--where employees can speak freely with different members of management. Unfortunately, the open door is too often a breeze-through. Employees come in, says their piece and the grievance breezes right on through--nothing is ever done about it.

In that case, the open door provides a safe conduit, but an ineffective one. Failure to follow through is another way of devaluing employees. Employees will quickly cease to use the open door, not because it isn't available or safe, but because it is meaningless. Your concern for the welfare of your employees and your stated belief in their worth appears to be just so much hot air. Your vibration of appearing to "do something" with no real action taken matches up with the employee's vibration of appearing to do their job without really committing wholeheartedly.

If you're going to have an open door policy, make it real. Few actions speak louder to employees of your genuine valuing of their well-being than your willingness to hear and do something about employee grievances. It's not that employees have to always have their way. It's more a matter of actively addressing that grievance, even if the way in which you do it is different from how the employee envisaged the solution. If you can't do anything about the grievance, then support a vibration of sincere valuing of the employee by explaining truthfully (not simply justifying!) why you can't.

A SUGGESTION BOX THAT WORKS

The same holds true of the suggestion box. A suggestion box is a great device for learning all sorts of things employees are uncomfortable talking about without the protection of anonymity. However, if the suggestions offered are rarely discussed or implemented, employees lose faith in the company and believe, once again, lip service is being paid to their contribution instead of genuinely valuing their ideas.

A genuine, well-tended suggestion box, like a genuine, effective open door policy, has a whole host of benefits. Besides contributing to the increased psychological well-being of employees, employees are often the ones best suited to suggesting valuable changes and innovations.

Southwest has seen the value of the suggestion box in many ways. Jones and Stone of SWA recount that: "We have low turnover, high Employee morale. Very happy Employees who feel more like owners of the company than Employees. They aren't afraid to make suggestions. Recognition comes from leadership down, but feedback comes from the bottom up. Feedback from our Employees is welcomed, encouraged and sought after. They are out there with the Customers and see what is working well and what can be improved.

"While Southwest doesn't have a physical 'suggestion box,' the airline's open door policy encourages Employees to make suggestions of all kinds -- covering everything from operational procedures to the cost of paper towels at Southwest's corporate headquarters building!"

Valuing your employees by giving them the opportunity to express themselves entrains valuable suggestions and ideas from your employees.

If you want to add even more value to the suggestion box, every time you implement one of the suggestions, have a banner, bulletin board or large company wide announcement of the "Hurrah! Another suggestion box idea helps us continue to achieve excellence!"

Employees: the Great Divide

Whether such an announcement includes the name of the offering employee depends on whether the suggestions are anonymous or, if identified, if the employee wants public recognition. In either case, loudly applauding the worth of the employee suggestion increases the general vibration of appreciating your employees.

ENCOURAGE TRAINING AND CLASSES

Encourage appropriate training and classes. Let employees know how valuable they are by investing in their ability to either do their job better or further their career within the company.

"Our company's great about giving us the time--and paying for--us to go to classes and seminars. It's one of the things I like best about working here. Our bulletin board is always filled with classes and training you can take.. And if you know of a class that isn't on the board, you can ask and most of the time, they'll let you take it and pay for it too. I've received all sorts of specializations over the years. I'm a nurse and it makes my work much more interesting. Plus, I come back recharged and full of ideas. I know I do a better job because of it.

> "I feel really good about working here because I feel like they care about me as a person. They support my growth and expansion. And it isn't just our department. It's the same throughout the whole center. If you're out to better yourself, they're all for it, whether you're in administration or on the floor. It's a good system."
> Peter V., RN

When you invest in your employees, not only do you support their well-being, but you also entrain a vibration of greater investment on their part in their job.

SHARE COMPANY INFORMATION

Share information about the company—where it is headed and future challenges and objectives. When people feel they are part of the bigger picture, they feel more valuable. A lack of information is tantamount to saying "You don't matter. There's no need for you to know this."

> "I'm a customer service rep for an on-line catalogue company. Day in and day out all I do is deal with customer questions and complaints. Which is fine. I like dealing with people, even cranky ones! But new catalogues come in and others go out and I never know

why or what's going on. If I ask, I'm just told, 'You're here to answer customer questions and complaints. You don't need to know anything else.' That's all. I don't know why, but that feels demeaning. After a while, it's demoralizing. I used to come in all charged up, now it's pretty much 'another day, another dollar,' and that's it."
Adele M., customer service representative

Sharing information empowers employees; they feel worthwhile because they are being trusted with information beyond their immediate scope. Valuing your employees in this way supports good teamwork and facilitates cooperation.

"We're a clothing manufacturer. Nothing fancy, the kind of clothes you buy at Target or JC Penney. Once a week we have this big meeting. All of us are jammed together in the cutting and manufacturing area. The boss tells us exactly what is going on. She talks about what order just came in and isn't it great we landed a fall line for Kmart or whatever, how our pattern makers broke all their own records for accuracy last week, or how we're bidding on this great new fabric. Our boss manages to say something about each department, from designers to drivers about what's new, what's going on, and she gets us all revved up.

"It's not always good news. Sometimes we didn't get a contract, or we had a large number of returns, but our boss somehow makes you feel like these are just opportunities to make our whole company better. She has faith in us to do that, like we're the reason the company will continue to do well. She makes us all feel like a somebody. It's not usually like that in the garment industry. At other companies I've worked for, it's 'do this and do that and don't waste my time asking questions about why.' I couldn't go back to that now."

Saul C., accountant

APPRECIATION SUPPORTS EMPLOYEE HEALTH AND WELL-BEING

Appreciating who your employees are and what they do has enormous impact on their level of happiness, which in turn directly affects their health and well-being. Employee health and well-being translates into dollars for you, in both obvious and less obvious ways. Obvious ways include decreased absenteeism, more energy, less downtime and lower turnover. Less obvious are better morale, greater enthusiasm, better focus, less depression, better motivation-- all of which can suffer when people are physically ill or emotionally under the weather.

Happiness is a natural consequence of feeling valuable, doing meaningful work and having that work acknowledged gratefully. Appreciating your employees is how you can contribute to that happiness.

Happiness is directly related to optimism, which has been the subject of rigorous studies. For example, long-term studies have shown that heart-disease rates among men who describe themselves as optimistic are fully half the rates for non-optimistic men. Optimists have better pulmonary function as well, which is highly significant since poor pulmonary function is an indicator of a number of problematic health issues including premature mortality, pulmonary and cardiovascular diseases. People who are hopeful and curious, traits that are characteristic of optimists, suffer less from hypertension, diabetes and upper-respiratory infection.

Optimistic people are less subject to stress, and therefore respond better in stressful situations. Happy people are less prone to depression and hostility. Numerous studies have shown that happy people take better care of themselves; they are more likely to exercise, have regular medical checkups, and take advantage of preventive health measures.

The upshot of all this, is that a happy employee has much

greater likelihood of being a healthy employee with all the associated advantages physical and emotional health and well-being signify in the workplace.

Happy employees will take that happiness and well-being home. Their ability to deal with the normal stressors of home life is likely to be greater, since happy employees are not as emotionally depleted at work as would be the case if they were unappreciated. The probability of having an awake, focused, energetic employee walk in to work every morning are thus greatly increased.

"Our boys are teenagers now--15 and 17, and my wife works too, so coming home after work is always hectic. I never know who the kids are having over, how many will be there for dinner, who's in trouble at school or what crisis my wife had to deal with that day. Then there's the usual, you know – bills to pay, things around the house to fix , the dog throwing up, things like that.

"Well my old supervisor was a real bear. He'd stress us with way too much work to do in too little time, yell at us for not getting it done, was never available to help, and generally was critical and on our backs all the time. I'd get home jittery and irritated and I'd have to make a big effort not to take it out on the wife and kids. I found it difficult to deal with the kids' noise and commotion, and the least little thing would set me off. I slept miserably. I'd toss and turn, and I'd be grumpy in the morning. I got sick a lot - it seemed I'd get one cold after another. My digestive system was a mess.

"Well, our supervisor dropped dead of a heart attack. I'm not surprised. Frankly, he was always red-faced and angry. Anyway, the new guy they brought in has a completely different style. He doesn't overload us with work, or if he does, he finds ways to help us do it. He's real supportive and tends to ask 'How can I help?' instead of 'Whaddya want?' or 'Get outta here, I'm busy.'

"My wife tells me I'm a lot easier to deal with, and I've noticed I'm actually whistling sometimes on the way home from work. I have a good feeling of accomplishment at the end of the day. The kids' ruckus doesn't bother me as much. I haven't had a cold in months and the only time my digestive system kicks up is if I've overdone the chili. I sleep better, too, which is probably why I don't come in all grumpy in the morning."
Fred H., airplane mechanic

The Power of Appreciation in Business

Appreciation is a terrific win-win. It's a win for employees who feel better about themselves, their job, and who enjoy better health and well-being, both physically and emotionally. It's a win for your business, for a healthy and happy employee can function at that level of performance and productivity you desire.

CHAPTER 4

MANAGERS: BETWEEN A ROCK AND A HARD PLACE

MANAGING PEOPLE VERSUS MANAGING SYSTEMS

Managers must, on one hand, manage systems (budgets, quotas), and on the other hand, manage people. The two require very different skills. Too often, managers are well versed in managing systems, but do not do nearly as well managing people. Yet, as is all too obvious, keeping employees motivated, enthusiastic and effective is critical. Only in the presence of such a dedicated workforce will your company thrive.

Managers, wanting to keep the company performing well -- not to mention keeping their job, are caught in a difficult situation. Their perception of how to keep employees happy is often at odds with their perception of how to keep "the boss" happy. Typically, systems will be managed effectively and quotas and budgets met but at the cost of high turnover and employee "problems." This doesn't have to be the case.

If mangers succeed at synchronizing the company's performance and productivity expectations with those of the people who report to them, both systems and people fit together harmoniously. The key is to synchronize those expectations--and appreciation is what does this best.

Managers who value their employees and demonstrate that valuing through their own behavior are best able to synchronize expectations and, in turn, earn the trust and respect of their workers. Unfortunately, studies show that employees frequently look for new jobs at new companies, not because they dislike their current jobs, not even because they don't like their present company, but because they can't stand their manager. What managers think are "personality conflicts" are more often than not the response of under-valued employees. Such workers feel used and abused by their manager and as a result, don't trust or respect him or her. Employees cannot work effectively under these conditions. As a result, nothing works well; the business is out of sync.

Here are specific ways managers can better appreciate and value employees to the maximum benefit of the business.

Managers: Between a Rock and a Hard Place

BE YOUR BEST TO ENTRAIN THE BEST

Vibrations entrain (attract) like vibrations. If you want the people you manage to show up on time, have a good attitude, approach problems eagerly and pitch in when needed, you must show up on time, have a terrific attitude, enthusiastically attack problems and pitch in. You are valuing your people by being your best for their benefit. You are also entraining from them a vibration of "being my best."

>"My last manager was a downer. Seriously! He'd come in all grumpy and complain until he had his first cup of coffee. He had a scowl on his face all the time, like he was annoyed. The only time we saw him was when he was mad about something. Which was a lot. The picture I have in my head of my old manager is him walking away from me, the back of his hand waving in the air, and him saying 'Handle it.' My new manager is a completely different story. He's upbeat and real positive. He's on the floor a lot, with his shirtsleeves rolled up--always ready to help you with whatever you need.
>
>"He has this routine where every morning at 8:45 we start with a meeting in the lunchroom. Everybody takes turns bringing doughnuts--including him. And

he gives us a kind of pep talk. He tells us what he expects from us for the day, lets us know the good that happened yesterday and gets us all charged up for the day. What's funny is I used to be late a lot, but the meetings are so much fun, I actually get there early! A lot of us do. It's just a whole different feeling. I have more energy, I get more done. Our manager makes work a great place to be."
Teresa L., secretarial pool

Your "best" must be sincere and consistent. A more intense vibration entrains less intense vibrations, so your "best" must be sufficiently dedicated and persistent to be effective.

DON'T IGNORE THE BASICS

Appreciation is quickly and easily demonstrated with a few behavioral basics.

Say "please" and "thank you"

Both go a long way in letting those you manage know you appreciate them. As simple as it may be, attending to such civilities makes a big difference to employees. You are valuing your workers when you say "please" and "thank you" as part of your normal speech pattern instead of the demanding, "Do this now." Vibrationally speaking, "please" and "thank you" readily entrain appreciation because of long-standing connotations of such words in our culture.

> "I know I'm supposed to do a good job and I suppose it shouldn't matter if I get thanks for it, but it really does matter to me that my manager says 'thank you' when I hand him a report or tell him an idea. It makes me feel like a person. Like he's giving me respect. And when you give me respect, I'm going give you respect back."
> Harold R., systems analyst

You will be amazed at how many things you can find to thank your workers for when you make appreciation not just an occasional extra, but an obsession, when you deliberately engage the vibration of valuing and being grateful for your people:

- "Thank you for your attention"

- "Thank you for your patience"

- "Thank you for listening to me"

- "Thank you for your thoughts"

- "Thank you for your input"

- "Thank you for taking the time"

- "Thank you for your effort"

- "Thank you for following through"

- "Thank you for reminding me"

- "Thank you for helping out"

- "Thank you for being so prompt"

The list is virtually endless. As with all other aspects of appreciation, the more targeted, immediate and sincere your expression of thanks, the more intense and effective your vibration.

Look people in the eye when you speak

Eye focus reinforces value. Eye focus lets people know that they are of significance to you. People falling in love stare into each other's eyes endlessly. Let your people know that who they are and what they have to say is of value to you by looking them in the eye when you speak or are spoken to.

Managers: Between a Rock and a Hard Place

Call workers by name

Names are important. Names matter. Using a person's name says, "You are not just a number to me, you are an individual and I recognize you as such."

> "My supervisor looks me squarely in the eye and says my name when he talks to me. I'll tell you, I pay a lot more attention to him because of it. I used to have this other supervisor; he'd just sort of throw stuff at you and never looked up from his desk. I don't think he even knew my name. I was just a 'Hey, you.' I wouldn't walk an extra mile for that guy, that's for sure."
> Josh P., computer technician

Smile

Managers are often afraid to smile, fearing that it's unprofessional or sends a message of "all is well," causing people to slack off. Hardly. When you smile as you greet an employee or as you give praise, you are conveying appreciation. The appreciation will be felt. Smiling must be genuine. As with all appreciative behaviors, a smile simply plastered on your face for the sake of smiling will not have the desired vibrational impact.

The Power of Appreciation in Business

CATCH PEOPLE IN THE ACT OF DOING SOMETHING RIGHT

Most people worry when they see their manager looking over their shoulder or stopping by their work area. They are convinced that the manager is looking for something they did wrong. That very worry will often vibrationally entrain something done wrong!

Get your employees in the habit of anticipating your visits as an opportunity to be appreciated. When workers know you will be on the lookout for good work, their vibration will be entrained towards "good work" with the consequent positive results.

If you expect to catch workers in the act of doing something right, you will be met with good work most of the time. Studies show that a manager's expectations have tremendous impact on employee job performance. This makes perfect sense when you look at it from a vibrational point of view. Expectation is based on appreciation, it says: "I see your value, and because I see that worth so clearly, I have faith in your ability to perform to the level of that worth." This powerful vibrational message is almost invariably met with a strong positive response.

> "I remember the first time my manager gave me a difficult piece of work to do. He said, 'I know you can do this, Gloria.' He was new at the time, and I wasn't about to let him pull one over me. I came right back

at him with 'Oh, yeah? What makes you think I can do this?' He didn't miss a beat, he said, 'You showed on the last project that you understood the software. You used it well and you weren't afraid of taking a chance and getting creative with it. This is the same software, Gloria, just a different application.' Then he smiled this big old smile and said, 'That, Gloria, is why I know you can do it.'

"Well you could have knocked me over with a feather. I was tickled pink. I said, 'All right then.' You better believe I did that piece of work--nicely too, and faster than I thought I could."
Gloria T., office manager

Jones and Stone of Southwest Airlines talk about the leadership training which is held once a quarter. They state that; "We specifically teach them [managers] how to recognize people - that recognition is important. And we give them incentives to use such as our LUV Pats cards. These have messages on them…pat on the back cards. They're inexpensive but our Employees really like them. I've seen them displayed on their cubicle walls."

HOW TO GIVE APPRECIATIVE COMMENTS

Appreciative comments in the workplace can readily be misinterpreted as attempts at manipulation or as just plain "phony." Saying, "You're great" to someone may be heard as genuine once or twice, but not if said on a regular basis. "You're such a nice worker" can feel condescending, and "You're the best" is hard to believe when it's said to many people. In order to be effective, appreciation must be expressed in immediate and focused terms. Global expressions ("You're great," "You're the best") are not specific enough. Personal expressions ("You're such a nice worker") do not focus on the work.

Appreciative comments should be descriptive and specific: "The way you summarized the Smith meeting in your report was very concise, very helpful. Thanks." "Fixing the timing mechanism so quickly got us back on track for that big order. Thank you." Employees know what is valued and why. The comment is not manipulative or phony.

Personal expressions do not address what was appreciated or of value in the work, and thus are often embarrassing or off putting to the employee. They are not appropriate in the workplace. It may take you more effort to think of a specific comment, but "Thank you for helping Sarah finish her project," is far more valuing than "You're such a nice worker."

Managers: Between a Rock and a Hard Place

BE A PART OF, NOT APART FROM

Managers who remain aloof from their employees, lose. They fail to create the relationship of trust and respect so critical to employee morale, motivation and performance. Your implicit message to those you manage must be "I am willing to work shoulder to shoulder with you." It's a demonstration of your belief in the worth of your employees' endeavors. . Be a part of the team, not above it.

> Southwest Airlines works with the concept of "Servant Leadership," which according to Jones and Stone, is one who "sees his primary goal as serving fellow Employees--regardless of the need, regardless of title. It is to lead by example and to facilitate the success of fellow Employees by providing them the support, tools, training and encouragement they need to move forward."

> Stone talks about an Employee who was not only "hired for attitude and trained for skill" but who was also a natural "servant-leader;" "Mike Ryan is currently a senior director in ground operations. Mike came to Southwest Airlines in 1986 as a mail clerk--job sorting and delivering mail throughout Southwest's headquarters building. In fact, he delivered my mail. Mike's attitude and aptitude--and because he was

a servant leader--have been responsible for his rise through the ranks to senior management. He has learned the skills for each job he applied for on the way up, but his attitude of serving others and providing the tools they need to get the job done are what make him a great leader. You can't really teach that."

Angelicola, of Professional Cutlery Direct, says of his and other managers' involvement with employees; "We do ongoing training even with seasonal folks to help them provide outstanding service to our customers. We use role-play techniques with our employees. where I'll play the customer or vice-versa. And we quiz each other, not like a classroom, but bouncing questions off each other. Getting feedback from our employees on what might work better."

Many managers fear that by working directly with those they manage, workers will lose respect for them. This is a legitimate fear, for indeed, if you drop all management poise and behave just like another employee, you will lose respect.

"Managers! I've had all kinds, from the type who just say 'Do it' and don't care what you've already got on your plate, to those who pretend to be your friend and want to dish the dirt with you. Why would I want to do that with a manager? I have to work under him, and that's enough.

"The best manager I ever had would give me a job to do, look me square in the eye and say, 'Can you do this, Ken? Do you need any help with this?' And if I said no, he'd respect that, clap me on the back, and be off. He'd come back in a day or so and ask how it's going, and if he saw I needed help, he'd get his hands dirty and be right in there with me. I always appreciated that. Not many supervisors know when to step in and when to leave you be. He was a real professional."
Arnie P., regional dispatcher

Maintain your employees' respect by focusing on assisting them to do better, keeping your focus on their value and worth. Stay attentive to the task at hand and keep your interaction professional.

Don't try to "buddy up" with those you manage by engaging in long-winded personal conversations, joking around or other such non-work oriented behaviors. Certainly, your demeanor can be pleasant and affable, but your guiding principle should be, "Is my behavior aligning with the vibration I want to entrain?" "Am I encouraging what is of value in this situation?"

SET YOUR PEOPLE UP FOR SUCCESS

Workers can't perform when they don't know what to do or how to do it. Managers who fail to let their workers know what they expect, or change what is expected without sufficient explanation, are setting their workers up for failure. Nothing demoralizes employees faster.

> "I was meeting my quota – which isn't the easiest thing in the world. I have to stay on task and focus good, and I was pretty happy about that. One day my manager came along and said I'm not working fast enough, and I'm like 'Excuse me? I'm meeting my quota. Yesterday I even went above it.' He said 'Yeah well, we've got new quotas,' and I'm like 'Since when?' He said, 'Last week.' But you know, he never tells us anything, so I'm not real surprised he forgot to tell me. Anyway, I said to him 'How am I supposed to meet this new quota when I'm straining to meet the old quota?' He said 'Your problem, buddy, not mine. Just do it,' and leaves. Fat help he is."
> George B., sales representative

Value your employees by giving clearly stated tasks and objectives. If job duties and goals change, let the employees involved know what the changes are and why they are necessary. Workers are remarkably accepting of change when they understand their necessity and remarkably resistant when they don't. When you give new objectives or tasks, make sure your workers are on the same page. Just saying, "Get Project A finished" doesn't mean your workers know what you mean by "finished," or how all the pieces of "Project A" fit.

When you truly value your people, you will ensure that they have the tools, training and sufficient time to accomplish their tasks and meet company goals. Check in with your staff to make sure they are on track. If they aren't, it is your responsibility to work with them or with the company so they have what they need to successfully do their job.

> "One of the things I like about my supervisor is she never talks down to me. If I'm having trouble on a project, I can always go to her and ask for help and we'll go through it together. She never makes me feel like I'm stupid. Sometimes she'll put me with a more advanced tech for a few days so I can catch on and not worry that I'm going to make a horrible mistake and mess everything up. If I need new equipment, she goes to bat for me, or at least finds a way to make my equipment work better."
> Angie L., communications technician

Angelicola, of Professional Cutlery Direct, says; "As a manager, I try to be a part of the group, to get inside their head, know what they need . . . We talk to each other about how to best get a job done."

BE A PROBLEM SOLVER, NOT A PROBLEM CREATOR

Many managers unintentionally make problems more difficult to solve by blaming, making unprofessional personal comments or getting angry--all devaluing behaviors. These actions create resistance to problem solving. After all, if you've just called an employee "stupid" your vibration is one of "I don't value you." How can you expect the employee to value your next request? Vibration entrains like vibration.

> "I've never understood why managers think browbeating people is how to get things done. Calling me careless or worse isn't going get me to work better. It makes me feel terrible and I don't think as well when I feel terrible. Getting angry at me when I make a mistake is no help either.
>
> "Do managers think we make mistakes on purpose? When my manager gets mad at me, my stomach is in knots. How am I supposed to work better under those

conditions? It sure doesn't work on my kids, why would it work on us?"

Thea R., computer programmer

Asking "What do you need here?" "How can I help?" "Tell me how you see what's going on?" are all more effective than "Why can't you get it done?" "You're just too slow" or "You did it all backwards." A good rule of thumb is to ask "what, where, when and how" questions rather than "why" questions. Asking why tends to put people on the spot, and once again, vibrationally raises resistance.

Educate yourself about the problem instead of looking for whom to blame. When employees are unable to come up with a solution, and you give instructions to fix a problem, focus on educating the employee about the solution, rather than banging him over the head with it. An attitude of giving information is a valuing one and will entrain a valuing vibration in return.

> "If I had a school for managers I'd tell them to work with an employee to figure out why the person made the mistake, like asking 'What happened here?' instead of the manager assuming they know why. And figuring out what does the person need to learn to not make the mistake again. My sister's manager--she's like that. One time my sister was really tired and trying to get a rush job out. She left out some important documents.

"Well, after that, her manager sat down with her and they decided that before she sends out a rush job, she can check it with one of her co-workers. That took a lot of stress off my sister. Plus, she and her manager talked about how my sister can pace herself better so she won't get so tired. Now that's a good manager."
Mary Loo P., administrator

VALUE ALL YOUR PEOPLE

It's human nature to appreciate the people who do what we like and want, not those we dislike or are troublesome. Nonetheless, managers who fail to value all the people they manage cannot manage effectively. Playing favorites, applying the rules differently to different people, are ways of saying to those not in favor, "You don't matter, you're not worth much, I don't value you." Those who are in favor work in constant fear of falling from favor at the manager's whim. These are far from optimum working conditions.

Those who perform and produce at higher levels should certainly be rewarded and praised accordingly. That is not favoritism. When everybody knows what levels of performance must be reached to be rewarded, it's not about favorites, it's about performance. Such treatment is fair and will be responded to vibrationally as such. When workers know the rules and see those rules are applied across the board, it's fair. Fair is saying "You all have value, you all matter, you are all important." That's effective management.

There are, of course, times when the rules cannot be applied per usual. For example, an employee may have to be temporarily relocated from her cubicle to an office because of an allergic reaction to the paint used in the recent cubicle area remodel. Or an employee may be allowed flextime (when others are not) because of a sick child. In these rare cases, make sure that the reason for the change is made known so that other employees do not read the change as favoritism.

As difficult as it may seem, even the most ornery employee has something within themselves or their work that you can value. Do your best to align with what you value specifically about each employee, regardless of whether the employee is difficult or an even-tempered joy.

APPRECIATIVE LISTENING

Managers often think that managing people is about giving appropriate directives, motivating employees and fixing problems. Most of the time, managers try to reach these objectives by talking--and talking and talking. In truth, you will achieve a lot more, more effectively, by talking less and listening more.

Listening is a critical component of valuing. You cannot attend to what matters to your workers in the absence of appreciative listening. We often listen only for our side of the conversation: we listen for what we agree with, what we disagree with and what may help us prove our point. Instead, listen for the value within what the employee is saying.

For example, an employee says, "I can't get this work done on time." Typical responses might be;

- "Well, you'd better, because the client is waiting on you,"

- "You're so slow, I don't know what's wrong with you," or

- "Fine. Give it to me, I'll have so-and-so finish it up for you."

None of these responses make the employee feel valued. The first stresses an already stressed employee. The second and third responses undermine the employee's worthiness. Vibration entrains like vibration. A less valued employee will respond with a vibration of less value, meaning less competency.

Managers: Between a Rock and a Hard Place

Instead, listen for the value within the employee's, "I can't get this work done on time." You'll hear the value of the implicit "I want to get my work done on time." When you pay attention to the value within what the employee says, you are halfway home to remedying the situation.

In response to, "I can't get this work done on time," you could say, "I know you want to and I certainly appreciate that. Talk to me about what's in the way." You are not devaluing the employee. You've honored the implicit value in the employee's statement and opened the door to constructive problem solving.

Managers who toss out a disgruntled "Whaddya want?" when employees approach them cannot elicit value from their workers. A simple "How can I help?" or "What can I do for you, Tom?" asked without attitude, will result in a positive and valuable interaction.

Studies show that a manager who genuinely listens to employees without judgment, valuing who they are and what they have to say, ranks high with employees. Such appreciative listening builds trust and respect. Employees value these managers and listen to what they say in return. As a result, the manager is far more effective than one who fails to listen appreciatively.

How you listen tells your workers whether you value their

words. For example, listening without interrupting lets workers know that what they say is worth hearing all the way through. If you take notes while listening, you impress upon the speaker that you take what is being said seriously. We don't write down what's unimportant. When you set down whatever you were doing and don't allow interruptions in order to give full attention to the speaker, you let the speaker know that you value what he or she has to say.

Certain body postures and gestures let workers know they are being listened to. Maintain good eye focus with the speaker; keep your body language open and undefended (do not cross your arms over your chest, for example). Nod your head every so often, saying "uh-huh." These are commonly accepted non-verbal messages that say, "I am interested in what you are saying. What you are saying has value to me."

How you respond, even as you are listening, also lets workers know you value their thoughts. For example, say;

- "Sounds like you've been giving this a lot of thought,"

- "Tell me more," or

- "Sounds interesting, what else have you been thinking about?"

Managers: Between a Rock and a Hard Place

These are ways to reinforce your valuing your workers' words and support them in giving you more information.

Restating to make sure you understood what the speaker has to say is an additional way to value what you are hearing. For example, "OK, if I understand you correctly, you're losing time during the projection phase because the equipment keeps shorting on you," lets employees know you really were paying attention, and gives an opportunity to either continue with "Yeah, and that's not all" or to clarify with "Well, it's not so much that it's shorting out as …"

LISTENING TO EMPLOYEE GRIEVANCES

No one likes to listen to grievances, no matter who's expressing their distress. Managers typically dislike dealing with the emotional "messy" side of employee grievances. After all, it's one thing to be obliged to listen to your spouse's anger over something, quite another to have to sit there through an employee's outburst. However, failure to listen to that outburst can be to the detriment of your company. As pointed out before, allowing employees to express grievances safely is important to their psychological well-being on the job.

Because of their reluctance to deal with emotions, managers tend to overlook the employee's upset and go directly to the issue itself. Unfortunately, this approach just tends to increase the emotional component of the grievance, for the simple reason that the complaining person feels they have not been heard, and now ups the ante. A typical conversation might go as follows:

> The employee comes in agitated and exclaims:
> "I've just about had it. I came in this morning and my inbox is already full, and then I get everybody hounding me, "Gotta put a rush on this" "Get mine out right away" "Whaddya mean you're not done yet?" It's only 11:00 o'clock and I'm tearing my hair out!"
>
> The manager replies:
> "Calm down. It's no big deal. I'll take care of it."
>
> Employee (more heated):
> "Whaddya mean "calm down"?! This is insane!! I can't believe what they expect me to do – "
>
> Manager (interrupting):
> "I said, I'll take care of it."
>
> Employee (continuing, intense):
> "They just push me and push me –"

Managers: Between a Rock and a Hard Place

Manager (emphatically, cutting employee off):
"I'll take care of it."

Employee (peeved):
"Well you don't have to snap my head off."

At the end of this conversation, no one feels good. The employee is now further aggrieved by what is felt as an unsympathetic hearing by the manager. The manager is annoyed because he had to deal with an emotional scene that only went from bad to worse.

Telling someone to calm down before acknowledging his or her emotional upset is usually ineffective. There is a better way to approach such situations. If the manager appreciated the employee's emotional state, that valuing would entrain a vibration of appreciation from the employee, which in turn would make a constructive discussion possible. The conversation relayed above might then proceed differently:

The employee comes in agitated and exclaims:
"I've just about had it. I came in this morning and my inbox is already full, and then I get everybody hounding me, "Gotta put a rush on this" "Get mine out right away" "Whaddya mean you're not done yet?" It's only 11:00 o'clock and I'm tearing my hair out!"

The manager replies:
"It's a very frustrating situation."

Employee (a little less agitated):
"Yes! It's driving me nuts. "

Manager (nodding):
"That's totally understandable. It would drive anybody nuts. Now, let me see what I can do about it and I'll get back to you."

Employee (sighs):
"Well, OK. That would be great. Thanks."

Manager (escorting the employee out of his office):
"You're welcome. Thank you for bringing this to my attention."

Everyone leaves the situation feeling good. The employee feels that he has been heard, both in terms of his emotion and his issue. The manager took charge of the situation appropriately, both emotionally and issue-wise. The company benefits because the manager's and employee's expectations have been rapidly re-synchronized.

Notice that the manager did not say, "You're right" to the employee, take the employee's side, or launch into an emotional commiseration with the employee. The manager simply valued the employees feelings by acknowledging them in a third person format, "It's a very frustrating situation." The employee, appreciating the acknowledgement of his feelings, can let go of those feelings and shift his focus to his manager's problem-solving orientation. It is of course critical that the manager follow through on his promises.

ASK FOR EMPLOYEE OPINIONS

We often forget that the person best suited to speak about a job is the person who works that job. Managers who flat out ask employees "How could we do this better?" "What would make your job easier?" are rewarded with surprisingly useful information, especially when managers listen appreciatively. This encourages employees to give "the truth, the whole truth and nothing but the truth." When employee ideas are acted upon, manager value zooms in the employees' estimation. Their managers have responded in a valuable way to their suggestions, supporting the manager's belief in their value.

The highly motivating and powerful feeling of "we're all in this together" to create/deliver the best possible product is reinforced--all to the benefit of the company's bottom line. People commit more strongly to decisions affecting them when they've participated in the decision-making process. Asking for and genuinely listening to employee thoughts and opinions and implementing them wherever appropriate is a great way to support employee commitment to company directives.

Part of genuinely listening to employee comments is to check back with employees, and once again, ask, "Did this help make your job easier?" "Are things working better?" "Do we need to make further change?" Be open to whatever the employee replies. Always focus on listening for the value in worker comments. If an employee responds to your question with a "Yes, thanks," be sure to appreciate the thanks with appreciation of your own!

CHAPTER 5

CUSTOMERS: THE NECESSARY EVIL?

A NEW POWER DYNAMIC

There was a time when the way to gain customers was to make something they wanted. When you were the only game in town, that worked. If another company came along and produced a product similar to yours, you simply made yours better or cheaper (or both). You were then assured more customers. With the advent of a global economy, being the only game in town is nearly impossible. Making a better product or service becomes a marginal advantage. Wooing customers based on price eventually diminishes your profit margin to where you can't stay in business.

> "I used to think my business was about our product. We pride ourselves on our product being pretty darned good. As head of the company, I thought my job was

to see to it that we sold to more and more people. Sure enough, we built our market share and we're selling to a lot more people than we did 10 years ago.

"But in order to do so, we spend an inordinate amount of money on advertising. Plus, we have to keep cutting costs. We have to staff lean, and in the end, we're working twice as hard as we did 10 years ago and we're making less money. It doesn't make any sense to me. If this keeps up, in a few years we'll be selling a ton of product and the company will go bankrupt!"
Bill H., owner, electronic parts company

Welcome to the new economy where thriving means appealing to the customer with more than product and price. Customers now have such an array of choices when purchasing just about ANY product or service, that the power dynamic between customer and company has changed. The power now lies with the customer.

"I'm a contractor. It used to be that if I needed some new tools, I went to the local hardware store because that was the only place I could get tools. Then the big box stores came along, but it wasn't very different. If I wanted hardware, I could go to the local hardware store or I could travel a few extra miles to Home Depot. But now, buying almost anything is a whole new deal.

Customers: The Necessary Evil?

I don't just pop down to the local store or even Home Depot. I go online first.

"I look up whatever it is I'm interested in--a new power saw--let's say. I use the Internet to figure out what's the best brand. I look up what customers are saying about the tool. I'll then shop around for the best price. I'll even take into account the different delivery options. Whether I'm better off walking into an actual store or buying online, in the end, I feel like I'm in charge of what I buy and why. It makes me feel a lot better about spending my hard-earned cash."
Tim S., general contractor

Even in the area of such services as health care and insurance needs, customers are increasingly proactive, seeking out information as to which plan will bring them the greatest benefits, not only in terms of cost, but in terms of the experience afforded by different companies.

Considering how much people talk to each other via the Internet, good customer experiences with your product or service are more important than ever. It's more than just a neighbor telling another neighbor about the quality of your product and influencing a sale, it's the neighbor from across the globe telling the world!

No matter how your customer comes to buy your product initially, it's what happens after the sale that's important. Studies show that your customer's level of willingness to come back and buy from you again, to tell their friends and family to buy from you and thus to become a loyal customer is what determines your true profit.

IT'S ALL ABOUT THE EXPERIENCE

Customer satisfaction surveys were thought to be solid indicators of customer loyalty. In fact, customer satisfaction says little about whether customers will ever buy from you again or recommend your product or service to friends and family. Customer loyalty is predicated on something that goes way beyond mere satisfaction. Your customer's willingness to become loyal, and even more than that, to become an advocate for your product or service depends on the quality of the experience you afford the customer. That experience encompasses the purchasing process (including delivery), the product (performance, ease of function, durability) and how customer concerns were handled.

This is where appreciation makes all the difference.

Customers who feel appreciated in every aspect of their experience with your company respond with a vibration of appreciation for you. Their expectations of getting fair value for their dollar are now synchronized with your expectations of giving them that value. What matters to customers isn't the amount of dollars spent, per se, it's the synchronization of fair value. The experience Starbucks aficionados receive at their local Starbucks matches their expectation. The fact that they are paying three to four times what they would pay for a similar cup of coffee at the local coffee shop is warranted by that experience.

As you value customers, you entrain a vibration of value from them. That vibration of appreciation for your product and service grows, as with each new encounter the customer feels appreciated yet again. Like attracts like.

> "I wanted to give my husband something special for his birthday. He had these shirts he really loved, but they were worn and frayed at the collar and cuffs. I thought I'd get him a couple of new shirts by the same manufacturer. I went online and found the company that made them, but I was shocked by the price! These shirts were expensive, but I thought, well OK, my husband loves his old shirts so the price seemed worth it. I ordered two. When they arrived, I realized I'd ordered the wrong color for one of them. I called the company to order a new shirt in the right color. I knew it was my mistake, not theirs, so I was just expecting to put the order through.

"But when I told my story to the lady at customer service, she said, no problem, she'd ship the new shirt out right away--and she'd ship it express so my husband would get it in time for his birthday. She also said she wasn't charging me shipping because she was sorry I had to go through this. She asked me what kind of gift wrapping I'd prefer and if I'd like to include a card. Then she told me that she'd include a pre-paid return label so I could ship the shirt I didn't want back, free of charge. I was flabbergasted! She was really going out of her way to help me out and make things right. All this even though it was my mistake.

"Well, she made a believer out of me. I couldn't wait to tell my friends how great the company was, and I'm definitely buying from them again. They really know how to treat people right."
Helen R., customer

Valuing or appreciating your customer is far more complex than giving "bonus points" or having a customer service center. Appreciating your customer is part of a new paradigm, an obsession with value.

Customers: The Necessary Evil?

DELIVER ON YOUR PROMISES

Valuing the customer starts with delivering on your promises: if you say something will be there overnight, it had better be there overnight. If you say your product cleans even the stubbornest stains, it had better do so. Whatever you claim your product or service achieves for the customer, it must do. When your widget does what your widget was supposed to do, the customer's wants or needs have been respected, therefore the customer feels valued.

Customer response when you have consistently delivered on your promises is unmistakable. The benefits of customer loyalty translate into profits as well as into heightened employee motivation.

> Van Doren of See's Candies talks about how "Eleven years ago, we were sitting in a meeting with letters from people asking why we didn't have stores in the Midwest and the East Coast. I was just musing, "I wonder if we could have a cart,' and out of that came the idea for the stands in the malls and airports. I was out in Atlanta, Georgia at a stand, and I saw down in the mall these two ladies screaming and walking down our way. And I said to someone 'look at those ladies screaming." I looked past our stand on the other side to the doors of the mall but there was nothing going

on over there, and I looked back and those ladies were still screaming and coming right toward us. They were so happy to see a See's!

"We ended up selling them candy even though we weren't open yet. In Arlington, Texas, at a cart, I was talking with some employees. One of them said, "I'm from the Midwest and don't really know about See's but I've been in retail all my life. And I've never had a customer hug me before."

"Customers hugged employees for being there. I've never heard of that happening with any other company. I think that makes employees truly proud of the company."

The opposite, of course, is equally true.

"I bought a number of external CD burners for my shop. The sales rep assured me that the burners were compatible with our computers and software. We got busy and I didn't get around to installing the burners for a couple of months after they arrived. I tried to install the first one and found that it was not compatible with our system. I called the customer service line and was told the burners were compatible and I just needed to have the tech run through the installation with me. I called the tech line. It was busy. It was busy for the next hour at which point I got a voicemail asking me to leave a message and the tech would call back shortly.

"The tech called back two days later, after hours, and left a message to call him. I called him back first thing the next morning, and once again, I got a busy signal. This went on for another couple of days. By now, I was fed up and wanted to return the burners. I called customer service and was told I couldn't return the burners because returns are only accepted 30 days after the date of purchase.

"I am now not only out a fair chunk of change, I still need CD burners that work and I am furious. I feel I've been taken along for a giant ride and I resent the heck out of it. Will I ever do business with this company again? Are you kidding? Will I tell anyone who wants to hear about my miserable experience? You bet!" Harry B., owner, software company

Delivering on your promises is the very foundation of customer loyalty. You can have a spectacular restaurant setting and fantastic waiters but if the food isn't good, you won't develop loyal customers.

Quality control is critical to customer loyalty. Your obsession with value must pervade all levels of production or service including your quality control centers and other support staff.

Fuel your quality control center and other support staff with a willingness to operate at a high level by sharing customers' appreciative comments with them. If indeed your product is delivering what it promises, you will receive those comments. Making appreciative comments only available to salespeople, for example, is an unfortunate limitation of their entraining potential. When employees hear how customers value the product and staff contributions are widely acknowledged for a job well done, that appreciation entrains employee vibration of appreciation. This translates into an increased willingness to value what and how they do their job.

> "I'm a poultry inspector. We inspect chickens at the final stage before they get shrink-wrapped – or at least that's what I call it. We're down there doing the same thing, day in, day out, and it's hard sometimes to keep motivated and not let an inferior chicken slip by. One thing that helps a lot is whenever a store doubles its order, or a customer calls and asks where she can find our brand because somebody just won a cooking contest using our chickens, the higher ups make sure all of us hear about it – not just the guys in sales. We get to see some of the fun stuff. How our chickens are

faring out there in the world.

"It makes a difference to know that customers appreciate what we do. Makes me want to do the best I can on my end to makes sure that happens even more."

Chuck U., poultry inspector

GETTING TO KNOW YOU

Customer loyalty is an intensely individual matter. Each and every customer, be they a corporation or a homemaker, wants to feel that their individual needs are addressed. It really doesn't matter to Customer Smith if Customer Jones is happy. Customer Smith will become a loyal customer if he feels his needs are important to a company and his needs are specifically valued.

Southwest Airlines is acutely aware of how important the Customer is and go to considerable lengths to let the Customer know he or she is individually known. Per Jones and Stone; "We have a department of about 150 people that respond personally to Customer letters. Every Customer who writes a letter is responded to with an individual letter. This department responds personally to address a problem or answer a complimentary letter. We have no form letters here."

You can't value what you don't know. Companies gather huge amounts of data on their customers, but it usually tells them precious little about what those customers want. Certainly, companies consider demographic information when packaging a product to appeal, for example, to "soccer moms" or to "harried business people on the go," but these broad-based considerations are not enough. They may very well miss specific aspects that are valuable to customers. Customer surveys are helpful to a point, but most people - potentially many who can be your most loyal customers - have no inclination to fill out customer surveys.

Often the best source of information about what customers want is the questions customers ask about a product and the complaints they voice.

> "We're a children's clothing manufacturer. We regularly send reps out to the stores carrying our clothes to ask salespeople on the floor, 'What are shoppers saying about our clothes? What are they asking for?' We get all sorts of information we'd miss otherwise. For example, we brought out a line in the latest lime green color. The salespeople told us the moms loved the style but hated the color. They wanted pink or blue.

Customers: The Necessary Evil?

> "In another line, we were using Velcro as a fastener for the collars on a girl's coat. The salespeople said that girls were getting their hair caught in the Velcro so they were getting a lot of returns. That kind of feedback is invaluable. It definitely helps us stay in touch with what customers really want, not just what we think they want. I always make sure the reps thank the salespeople and let them know just how important they are to us--because they are!"
>
> Paul W., owner, children's clothing company

What you do with that information is what develops customer loyalty.

> "I manage the customer service department for our company. As you can well imagine, we handle a lot of complaints as well as general customer questions. My people log each caller by the problem or question. At the end of the week, I sort through the comments to track repetitive complaints or concerns so I know what needs to improve.
>
> "We have a department head meeting once a week where we discuss what I've found. We make decisions right then and there on how we can make our customers' experience better. I'm convinced that's

one of the key reasons for our success. We don't just handle customer complaints. We proactively use those complaints to make our product more valuable to our customers."

Sandy P., manager, customer service department

USE FOCUS GROUPS

Another great source of information about customers is the use of focus groups. Focus groups are frequently used to determine the validity of a new product, advertising campaign and other development issues, but far less frequently to determine how closely a product or service is aligning with what customers value—or don't value—about a product or service.

A focus group is simply a group of people similar in demographics to your customer, or to the customer you want to learn more about, hired to give their opinion on a particular matter.

For example, if you want to know how the new layout of your store is working for your customers, you could hire a group of demographically representative individuals for the day. You would pay them a reasonable fee for their time and have them spend the morning in your store looking for and purchasing various items. You would spend the afternoon asking them targeted questions about how easy or difficult it was for them to find the items, to navigate about the store and the purchasing experience. You would be astounded at the extremely valuable practical information you would soon discover.

"We hired a human factors consultant to help us design the new cashier configurations for all our stores. He showed us numerous scientific studies explaining the difference in human perception given different shapes and strategic positioning of the cashier areas. We got excited about potential improvement in traffic flow and the consequent increased sales volume. We made the changes in the first store--and watched our sales decline. I couldn't understand why. I checked the various departments and nothing had changed except the new cashier configurations.

"So, after hours one night, I kept the cashiers on overtime, and got a group of my friends together (with a promise of dinner afterwards!) to pretend they were customers. Within an hour, I discovered exactly what the problems were with the new cashier configurations. We were able to go ahead with the new configurations in the other stores with just the few changes suggested by my customer 'guinea pigs.' And yes, sales did indeed increase, much to our relief. Later, I found out I'd conducted a very non-scientific process called a 'focus group.' We've used focus groups in a more formal way since then and have always derived tremendous benefit."

Sally F., VP of Sales, pharmacy chain

The focus group doesn't have to be a group of individuals sitting in a room, as is traditionally the case with marketing or product development. You could have individuals in the group call your customer care center with a number of concerns and debrief them as to their experiences. Or, a focus group can use your product or service and provide you with "regular people's" opinions, something which truly is worth gold.

"We have a number of software programs including an anti-virus program. We wanted to check out the efficiency of our customer service department for beginning level users so we put together a focus group of people who were not computer savvy. One of them tried to install our product and his computer crashed. He couldn't access our free website help desk, obviously, so he looked on our packaging for a number to call.

"We had two numbers, both paying calls--one where you are charged a service fee per call, the other where you are charged by the minute. This fellow was incensed! Here he'd never even been able to install the program and already we wanted more money. He told us if this had been a real life situation, he would have returned the product and never bought from us again.

"You'd better believe we immediately installed an 800 hotline for first time installation problems. We gave it a three-month trial period, during which time we received many calls. Most importantly, our return rate dropped significantly. If we hadn't conducted the focus group, we would never have known about this problem because most returns don't include a note saying why, even though we provide a "comments" section on the return invoice. We were able to keep the 800 number as a 9:00 – 5:00 hotline, which is easy for us to staff and keep costs down. It was definitely worth the investment."
Chen C., CEO, software company

The more you know what is valuable to your customers, the more you can honor what they value. The more valuable you make your product/service to your customer, the more likely their loyalty. Vibration aligns with like vibration. It's scientific.

GETTING TO KNOW THE CORPORATE CLIENT

On the corporate level, when your company is bidding for a corporate customer to adopt their product or services, "getting to know you" can be a more direct, and therefore more effective, process. If possible, get permission to go to the heads of the various departments and ask, "What would you like to see with this kind of product/service?" "What would work best for you?" "How should the product/service be set up? Managed? Implemented?"

Ask the actual employees who would perform the hands-on operation or use your product or service: "What was the problem with the last product/service of this type?" "What do you hope this product/service will accomplish for you?"

Thoroughly explore the ins and outs of the context in which your product will be used, what it is supposed to achieve from the perspective of the users and how it should benefit the corporation's bottom line. Now you're in a position to customize your product so that it is a perfect fit with the corporation's needs and goals.

This approach is an extremely appreciative one. You are learning about what is valuable to the corporation and feeding directly into it. Your ability to provide the corporation with a valuable experience is directly proportional to what you have learned about the corporation and to your ability to create promises you are fully equipped and committed to deliver.

"I'm in charge of leasing and purchasing equipment for a chain of hospitals. We were looking to replace our copiers and started talking with a bunch of reps from different companies. Most of them told us about their latest and greatest equipment and how it would copy X pages per minute. They wanted to know how many copiers we'd need and all seemed to be working on getting us the best deal. Which was pretty much business as usual.

"Then one guy said, 'There are a number of options. Would you mind if I came down to one of your hospitals and took a look at how your current copiers are performing and maybe talk with some of the staff who use the copiers?' I was surprised but I said, sure and suggested he come to the hospital I work at--to keep an eye on him. I assigned an assistant to show him where our copiers were, stay with him and told him to stay out of the way of the doctors.

"Well, he sat down with our insurance staff, employees in records and anyone else who used the copiers. He asked them all sorts of questions on how they used the copiers and if they had their wish what would a copier do? How could it help them better do their job? He came back to me a couple of days later with the most comprehensive report on our use and needs for copiers I have ever seen. He proposed a number of different copiers, tailored to various departments and in different price ranges. He factored in service programs, regular maintenance – well, I could go on. But the bottom line is, there was no question I was going to give this fellow our business. He had gotten to know our needs and addressed them specifically.

"Did I end up spending more than if I had gone with one of the other companies? Yes. But our office performance and productivity soared: less equipment down time, less wasted employee time, less wasted materials, better accuracy. The copiers save us a lot of money in a lot of ways."
Rachel C., head of purchasing

COMBAT THE "US VERSUS THEM" MENTALITY

Building a loyal and ever expanding customer base requires a profound appreciation of the customer. "The customer is our business" is more than a truism; it is a wonderful, valued, cherished fact. Too often, a company's point of view is: "We're doing the best we can, if it weren't for all the trouble customers cause, we'd be fine," otherwise known as "us versus them."

This point of view trickles down to the employees in direct interaction with the customer, from sales rep to customer service department to delivery driver. The upshot is a vibration of annoyance, disdain or irritation, which entrains a vibration of the same from the customer. The result? Unhappy employees and unhappy customers. Hardly a winning proposition.

Instead, think of every interaction with a customer as yet another opportunity to bring them into the fold of those who value and appreciate your product. It's an "us and those who don't know they're 'us' yet" mentality, very different from the typical "us versus them." For that to occur, employees who interface with the public must already be convinced of the excellence of your product or service, the benefit to those who will buy it, and the joy of sharing that excellence with customers.

> Alpert, CEO of Professional Cutlery Direct, states flat out; "From our inception in 1993, we've built a unique culture which allows us to provide outstanding service to our customers, by recognizing that our customer satisfaction starts with empowered, motivated, loyal employees."

Professional Cutlery Direct's culture has been written about in such notable publications as INC magazine, Catalog Age, and the New York Times, among others.

Bringing customers into the fold is easy for employees steeped in the value of your product/service.

"I'm the main science teacher for a fairly large middle school. Every year I order supplies for all our science classes. In the last few years, I've mostly bought on line, but I always call to actually place the order since we usually get a school discount and they rarely have a place for that on the website. I'd been buying primarily from one company. Its product is pretty good and their prices are reasonable. It's a straightforward transaction. Then a friend of mine who teaches up north suggested I try another company that she really enjoyed buying from. I had no particular ties to the company I was used to, so I called the company my friend uses.

"What a difference! As I started telling the customer service person my order, she said 'Oh, your 6th graders are going to love this,' and she proceeded to describe what was special about the product, and did I know there was a added feature I could send in for,

for free, and on and on. She wasn't pushy at all. It was more like she tuned in quickly to what would benefit my class. She had an intimate knowledge of all her company's products and it was clear she just loved them! I felt like she wasn't treating me like a customer, she was treating me like someone special she wanted to share this wonderful product with.

"It was amazing--my friend was right. I had a great time ordering my supplies. I will definitely place next year's order with the new company. I'm going to ask them to suggest products for our other classes--I would trust their recommendation."
Jane P., middle school science teacher

An appreciative cycle leads to success and profits. It starts at the top. The CEO or founder of the company sees the value of, and appreciates intensely, the product or service. The CEO appreciates employees, vendors and others who make and distribute the product so those employees appreciate the product themselves. Appreciated and appreciative employees convey that appreciation to those who wish to buy it. Customers, in turn, become loyal customers, returning to buy more product and extolling the brand to friends and family. Truly a win-win.

REALITY CHECK

This win-win situation may seem to be a fairy tale. Your immediate response might be "And what fantasy world are you living in?" However, enough truly fine and successful companies have achieved this appreciative cycle to confirm its validity.

Take Southwest Airlines, for example. In an era where many airlines are filing for bankruptcy or are operating seriously in the red, Southwest is flying in the black just fine and luring repeat customers. Southwest enjoys a surprisingly large percentage of loyal customers whose appreciation of the airline directly reflects the appreciation its employees and management have for the airline and its customers. This is particularly significant because studies show airlines typically engender a very low ratio of emotional commitment from customers relative to other industries.

> "I'm a business traveler. I'm up and down our state at least two or three times a month. I started flying Southwest for the fares. They were a lot more reasonable than anyone else. At first, I really resented that open seating they do. I hated having to stand in line to try to get a good seat. But after a while, I realized I always got a decent seat, so it wasn't that big a deal. But what really got me was how friendly, upbeat, and helpful everybody is at Southwest. If you call them

about something, there's never a hold or that endless series of prompts you get on other airlines, you get a real live person right away. And they always seem happy to hear from you, which is very refreshing.

"The flight attendants are never snotty, they often make jokes and sing, and generally make the whole thing fun. But what I really appreciate about Southwest is the no-hassle factor. If I get to the airport early, I can easily get on standby for an earlier flight and I usually get on. If my meeting ran late and I didn't make my flight, they'll just pop me on to another one.

"I've had Southwest personnel bend over backwards to help me fly the way I want to, which is to say with the least wait-around time possible. What can I tell you? I've become a dedicated frequent flyer."
Mike K., regional sales manager

THE CONSCIOUS EMPLOYEE

Loyal customers will not blossom in the absence of an appreciative work force. Employees must be selected and trained to value customers.

"I've been shopping at this small natural foods store for years. They have wonderful organic produce and meats. They're pricey, but organic foods are important to me so I don't mind. The store must have done really well because they were bought out by a big chain of natural foods stores, and I must tell you--I don't like it any more. The food is the same, but the help is terrible! The checkers don't look at you; they're always talking to each other even when they're ringing up your order. If you ask them a question about a product, they just shrug and say, 'I don't know.' They look bored and uninterested.

"Oh, how I miss the help they used to have! The checkers and stock people knew everything in the store. They were helpful and always friendly and attentive. I don't get it. Why'd they fire all those good people and hire a bunch of employees who don't care? There's a new natural foods store opening up near my work. I'm going try shopping there. It's hardly worth paying these higher prices to get treated this way."
Debbie S., customer

Although a good fit between the employee and the job is important at all levels and in all departments, any employee who interfaces directly with the public has an added responsibility to

Customers: The Necessary Evil?

consciously, proactively and deliberately appreciate customers. Managers responsible for hiring these employees must consider this.

We all have different innate predispositions. It's easier to hire people who already have a good sense of people skills than to try to train those who don't. Psychological testing can help weed out potential employees who don't have such skills, as does good interviewing. However, the most effective way to determine who is best suited for direct contact with customers is a sufficient probationary period and a good mentor.

> "I supervise a call center for a major computer manufacturer so we get customer calls of all sorts around the clock. I think of myself as a pretty decent interviewer, but I've learned that the proof is in the pudding. When I need a new call-taker, I bring in four new hires at a time, put them through intensive training, give them a seasoned "buddy" to help them learn the ropes and a three-month probationary period. At the end of three months, I keep the best one or two call-takers. That's it.
>
> "It may seem a waste to hire four employees when I only need one or two, but my retention rate is excellent and our customer call center is ranked the best in the

company. In the long run, it works out financially very well."

Rick M., call center manager

TRAIN YOUR EMPLOYEES TO APPRECIATE

Support your employees' ability to appreciate customers by teaching them about vibration and how their vibration of appreciation can entrain customer appreciation. Training should include a number of do's and don'ts on what constitutes valuing behaviors . For example, using customer's names is a way of valuing them. Listening attentively and directly addressing customer's stated desires is another. Asking questions that show the employee appreciates what the customer values is yet another.

Failing to appreciate what the customer values damages the company's value to the customer.

"I don't understand some sales people. I was in a department store and told the sales person I wanted a long sleeved cream-colored sweater. She brought out a three-quarter sleeve tan sweater. The three-quarter sleeve didn't bother me so much, it's the style these days, and I thought, oh well, maybe 'cream' to me means 'tan' to her. I showed the sales girl a swatch from the skirt fabric that I needed to match, and once again, she put the tan sweater under my nose, saying, 'This is what we've got.' That didn't help me at all.

"I looked around and saw a cream-colored blouse with long sleeves that might work. I took it over to the sales girl and she said, 'You didn't say you wanted a blouse.' I thought, no I didn't, but goodness, if she'd asked me a little about why I was looking for a long-sleeved cream colored sweater, maybe she'd have thought of the blouse."
Bertha F., customer

Role-playing different customer situations with seasoned co-workers is a terrific way of showing new hires how to appreciate customers in a variety of situations. Training should demonstrate that there are a number of ways employees can value customers to get their appreciative vibration going.

"We manufacture printers. I handle calls from customers with technical problems. Most customers are nice people who are just trying to get their printer to work right. Those are easy to value because I can appreciate that they are nice people. They're usually very grateful when the problem gets fixed--which is most of the time. But occasionally I get a real doosey, you know, the screaming type of customer where you have to push your headphones off your ear so your eardrums don't pop out. I really couldn't appreciate anything about these customers. They're usually nasty from start to finish and more likely to end the call with 'It's about time' instead of 'Thank you.'

"Then my supervisor pointed out that these customers valued their work so much and wanted so badly to get on with it, that they were very frustrated when their printer wasn't working right. I started thinking about how frustrated I would be if my computer went down while I was trying to resolve something for a customer. That really helped.

"Now, when I get an aggravated customer on the line, I just take a deep breath and think how much this person really loves their work, and how much I want to help them get back to it. I still have to push my headphones off my ear--but I feel much better doing my job."
Ursula T., tech support

Appreciating customers requires energy and patience. No one feels upbeat all the time, yet any employee who interacts directly with the public must maintain an upbeat disposition and a goodly supply of patience. These are prime ways we demonstrate our appreciation of someone. Customers are not necessarily easy individuals to appreciate. As your employees set their vibration of valuing customers in motion, most customers will respond in kind. Vibration entrains like vibration. This makes the employees' job considerably easier.

Unfortunately, some customers have no vibration of appreciation within themselves (for whatever reason), and yet the employee must still value the customer as strongly and genuinely as possible.

Therefore, in addition to recognizing and overtly appreciating employees' good humor, positive energy, and whatever other valuing attitudes they demonstrate towards customers, it's important to give these employees an opportunity to "decompress." Whether it's in the form of individual attention or a group meeting, employees will benefit from an opportunity to vent whatever aggravation they feel in their interactions with customers. They should receive praise for how they handled difficult customers and provided suggestions for how to value such customers in the future.

> "I'm a field rep with a large company. We're always out there dealing the best we can with our accounts. Once a week, we all sit around with our supervisors and share the best and worst stories of the week. This

has nothing to do with how much business we booked. This is all about our interactions with the different accounts and how we fared. I have to tell you, it feels great.

"We get mutual pats on the back for our best calls, where we got something done even better than what the customer expected, and we get to moan and groan to each other about the worst calls--the customer who's never satisfied no matter how hard you try. Of course our supervisors tell us 'A miserable customer is just a happy customer in the making' and we all share ideas on how to make that happen. There's such a feeling of camaraderie between us; trying to make good customers of them all. It makes the job fun."
Irwin S., sales representative

APPRECIATE CUSTOMER COMPLAINTS

One of the easiest ways to develop loyal customers is to handle their complaints in a way that brings them back into the "I love this product" fold. For that, customer complaints should be seen as another opportunity to demonstrate how the company can appreciate their customers and not, "Here we go again, complain, complain, complain."

Customers: The Necessary Evil?

When problems arise, sufficient mechanisms need to be in place so that employees can respond quickly and easily to the most common complaints in a way the complaining customer finds valuable. Southwest Airlines, for example, makes it easy for a customer to change a flight at the last minute, thus responding to the complaining customer's "I missed my flight" or "I'm early, I don't want to have to wait" with virtually no hassle.

In addition, employees need sufficient tools and options to resolve less common problems in a way, once again, that the customer will find to be of value. Sometimes, that means absorbing a short-term loss in the interest of developing a long-term profitable relationship (i.e., no-hassle returns, a reduced fee for services). Companies are usually already familiar with this mode.

Other times, bringing a customer back into the fold means being finding a creative way to right a negative situation so it is meaningful to the customer.

> "I wanted to get a gift certificate for my wife's birthday at a very upscale store I know she loves, but doesn't shop at much because of the price. Heaven knows if I tried to pick something out for her, it'd be all wrong so a gift certificate seemed like a good idea. I called the store and asked about purchasing one. I was told

'Sorry, we don't do gift certificates,' and I thought, 'How odd.' So I went to the store's website and called the main customer service number.

"I told the person who answered the phone what I wanted to do. She couldn't have been nicer. She said, 'We don't do gift certificates usually, but I can't see why we wouldn't. I think a gift certificate is a great idea. I'll be happy to get one to you right away. I'll make sure the store will honor it.' She put me on hold for a minute, came back and said, 'No problem, they'd be delighted to honor a gift certificate.' The gift certificate came the next day, along with a card to go with it and a nice handwritten note wishing me a wonderful celebration for my wife's birthday. Now that's service."
Thomas B., customer

Southwest Airlines' Jones and Stone talk about how; "We allow Employees to make decisions regarding the Customer. We have a booklet called 'Guidelines for Leaders" which is just that. Guidelines, not rules. They can bend the "rules" to help the Customer. We encourage our Employees to be flexible, to do the right thing."

Customers: The Necessary Evil?

Stone continues with; "Everyday we have examples of Customer Service Employees who show compassion by refunding the fare on a nonrefundable ticket because it was "the right thing to do" in a particular circumstance, like death of a loved one. Or a flight attendant who helps a Customer celebrate a special event by waiving the drink charge on a flight."

Bringing customers back into the fold always means listening attentively, learning what is valuable to customers and providing that value. Companies would benefit by training employees how to answer customer problems in this way and by giving employees both the means and the latitude to be creative.

"You know for us it's pretty simple. I'm a customer service rep, and I have a certain amount of money I can spend on callers in a week. I can spend it on free shipping for the customer, on adding an item to their shipment, on upgrading a service – we have a long list of appropriate give-aways, each with a "price tag."

"Now the challenge our supervisor gives us is, how creative can we get with these give-aways so the customer walks away happy, but we haven't used up our allotment for the week. The money we don't use on customers goes into a kitty that ends up as prize money to the rep who has the most callers come back and buy more from the company. It's pretty exciting. Keeps us on our toes, that's for sure."

Ben D., customer service representative

CULTIVATE THE CUSTOMER'S EXPERIENCE

Customers want to feel special. They want to feel valuable. They want their experience of your product or service to be meaningful to them. Customers don't care about anybody else's experience, only theirs--and perhaps that of friends and family. Cultivate your customers' experience in every way you can, making them feel special and valuing their unique needs, concerns, problems and desires.

Cultivating the customer's experience can go from the simple to the very complex.

See's Candies has a simple, yet very impactful way of cultivating the customer's experience. Van Doren says; "With customers the most obvious is the free samples. Everyone who comes into the store will get a free sample. We've been doing that since 1921. That puts a smile on the customer's face and has a reverse action for the employees. They've made someone happy which makes the employees feel good. And it makes the customers more comfortable. We want them to be happy when they come in. It's a candy store."

A bank customer has this to say:

"I know this sounds silly, but every year I get a birthday card from my bank. What I like about it is that the card doesn't have any advertising on it. It's not a come-on to use more of their services, or anything. It's just a nice picture on the front of some local nature thing, and inside it says, 'Happy Birthday from your friends at' and the name of our bank. That's it. It's really nice. Makes me feel special."
Andrea P., bank customer

Southwest Airlines' way of cultivating the Customer's experience is more complex and highly individualized.

Per Jones and Stone; "For our Customers, we have a monthly on board magazine where we feature Customers who fly with us a lot. Their names are submitted by Employees. We highlight Customers who are interesting, colorful, how flying Southwest has helped them. Several business men who fly Southwest have told us they grow their business based on Southwest's route map. They set up their businesses in our hub cities because they can get there on time and inexpensively. We also have Customer Appreciation Days in airports. Our Employees will have a laminator to make free baggage tags out of business cards for our Customers. We'll have games and prizes and massages available for free."

Pelletier, CEO of the Pelletier Group, has a unique way of thanking clients after a consulting job. He responds to "It's all about you, the customer" by giving clients a set of director's chairs which do not sport the consulting firm's name or logo, but rather the client's name. The client feels special and personally valued, because he is given a gift which is not an excuse for placement of a promotional item. Yet you can be sure that at least on several occasions, when the client is asked, "Gee, where did you get those nice chairs?" he'll answer with the name of the consulting firm. By valuing the client, the client values the firm.

Employees must be given the means and freedom to be creative within the limits set by the company. This is where customer oriented training is essential, both to help employees recognize and develop opportunities to value customers and to learn how to do so appropriately.

Customers: The Necessary Evil?

"I run an animal supplies shop. Of course we have people who buy off our website as well. In the 'comments' part of the web order form, people will often write about a problem they're having with their animal or some aspect of animal training or grooming. It took a bit of doing, but I've trained our staff to respond to those comments with something substantive, such as sending a sample of a product that might help or an article about what other people have found useful.

"People will come back to us telling us how helpful our response to their comments were, and often how surprised they were at getting a response in the first place. It certainly makes for a lot of repeat business."
Karen C., owner

Valuing customers creatively can have an immediate benefit as well.

"I run a specialty coffee shop at the airport. Usually we're jamming, especially in the mornings, and we hardly have time to breathe, much less get creative. But we had a slow afternoon last week so I sent some of my people out with trays full of small paper cups of our latest coffee creation and had them offer it to people waiting to board their planes. No pressure, just 'Thought you might like a little refreshment while you wait.' The response was terrific! Just about everybody said something like 'Oh, that's so nice, thank you!'

"From their expressions, you knew it was unexpected. People hand out freebies in supermarkets, but at an airport? Some people just drank their freebie and that was it, but quite a few said 'This is good' and walked up and bought a cup. For about the cost of a pot of coffee, I sold well over 20 cups at full price. I'm sure there were people who were experiencing our coffee for the first time that day. With any luck, they'll be back. I'd say that's not a bad deal for a slow hour."
Derrick C., manager

THE CUSTOMER IS YOUR BUSINESS

Scenario #1:
The customer books a booth at your exposition. He calls three days later and asks, "Do you know a videographer? I need some special effects shot for my display." You are not in the business of videos. You say "Sorry, can't help you there." The customer is OK with it. He didn't really expect much more.

Customers: The Necessary Evil?

Scenario #2:

The customer books a booth at your exposition. The customer calls three days later and asks, "Do you know a videographer? I need some special effects shot for my display." You are not in the business of videos. Nonetheless, you say, "Let me work on that. I'll get back to you in a day or two." The customer is surprised and happy. You make a couple of calls; get a recommendation for a good videographer from a friend. You call the client back. He's now delighted.

Three days pass, the customer calls, "Say, I'm wondering if you could recommend a computer graphic artist? That videographer worked out really well." You don't say, "Look, buddy, I got better things to do." You realize the customer is beginning to rely on your advice. You have more value for the customer than you did before. You say, "Let me work on that." You make a couple of calls; give your customer the name of a reputable graphics artist. The customer is impressed. He becomes a repeat booth-renter and brings new business to you as well.

In the space of the extra 10 or 15 minutes it took out of your day to make those calls, you greatly enhanced the customer's experience of your product. Over time you collect a file of "good service providers" so you can respond to customer needs easily and graciously without putting a strain on your time. You do this because you do not see your business as just renting booth space. You correctly perceive your business as taking the best care of customers as you possibly can. You recognize, correctly, that booths aren't your business, customers are.

When that attitude prevails throughout your company, through every department and employee, you are truly entraining customer loyalty. Because of that loyalty, yours will be a thriving business.

Staying in Touch

→ Do you have a **real-life appreciation story** to share?
> *Submit your appreciation success story to info@powerofappreciationinbusiness.com.*

→ Do you want to continue to learn to use **appreciation techniques** in your business?
> *Check out www.powerofappreciationinbusiness.com for a fresh appreciation tip every week!*

→ **Consult** with Dr. Nelson and discover how to better value your employees and customers to achieve higher productivity and sales!
> *For consulting information, please email info@powerofappreciationinbusiness.com*

→ Would your organization or business benefit from an appreciation message in a **keynote presentation** or seminar/workshop setting?

> To book Dr. Noelle Nelson,
> contact: Diane Rumbaugh
> Rumbaugh Public Relations
> email: rumbaugh@earthlink.net
> tel. (805) 493-2877

Thank you! We appreciate your interest in
THE POWER OF APPRECIATION IN BUSINESS.

www.powerofappreciationinbusiness.com

REFERENCES AND RECOMMENDED READING

REFERENCES

For an in-depth discussion of the science underlying appreciation's power, as well as the many additional ways and areas of life in which appreciation can be highly beneficial, please see:

Nelson, Noelle & Jeannine LeMare Calaba. *The Power of Appreciation: The Key to a Vibrant Life*. Beyond Words Publishing, Oregon, 2003. www.powerofappreciation.net

Institute of HeartMath ® Research Center
14700 West Park Avenue, Boulder Creek, California 95006.
www.heartmath.org - research and education
www.heartmath.com - programs

References and Recommended Reading

The Jackson Organization
Survey research consultants
6996 Columbia gateway Drive, Suite 202,
Columbia Maryland 21046
www.jacksonorganization.com.

RECOMMENDED READING

Annunzio, Susan Lucia. *Contagious Success*. Portfolio, New York, 2004.

Blanchard, Ken. *Customer Mania*. Simon & Schuster, New York, 2004.

Blanchard, Ken & Spencer Johnson. *The One Minute Manager®*. William Morrow, New York, 1982.

Burley-Allen, Madelyn. *Listening: The Forgotten Skill*. John Wiley & Sons, New York, 1995.

Calloway, Joe. *Indispensable: How to Become the Company That Your Customers Can't Live Without*. Wiley, New York, 2005.

Childre, Doc & Howard Martin, *The HeartMath Solution*. Harper, San Francisco, 1999.

References and Recommended Reading

Coffman, Curt and Gabriel Gonzales-Molina. *Follow This Path.* Warner Business Books, New York, 2002

Covey, Stephen R. *The 7 Habits of Highly Effective People.* Fireside, New York, 1990.

Covey, Stephen R. *The 8th Habit: From Effectiveness to Greatness.* Free Press, New York, 2004.

Ferrazzi, Keith (with Tahl Raz). *Never Eat Alone: And Other Secrets To Success, One Relationship At A Time*, Currency, New York, 2005.

Keller, Jeff. *Attitude is Everything.* INTI Publishing, Florida, 1999.

Kohn, Alfie. *No Contest.* Houghton Mifflin, New York, 1992.

Nelson, Noelle. *Winner takes All: Exceptional People Teach Us How to Find Career and Personal Success in the 21st Century.* Perseus, New York, 1999.

Pelletier, Ray. *It's All About Service.* Wiley, New York, 2005.

Peters, Thomas J. & Robert H. Waterman. *In Search of Excellence.* Warner Books, New York, 1982.

References and Recommended Reading

Sanders, Tim. *Love is the Killer App*. Three Rivers Press, New York, 2003

Sanders, Tim. *The Likeability Factor*. Crown Publishing, New York, 2005.

Selden, Larry & Geoffrey Colvin. *Angel Customers and Demon Customers*. Portfolio, New York, 2003.

Seligman, Martin E. P. *Learned Optimism*. Pocket Books, New York, 1998.

Sirota, David & Louis A. Mischkind, Michael Irwin Meltzer. *The Enthusiastic Employee*. Wharton School Publishing, New Jersey, 2005.

About the author . . .

Noelle C. Nelson, Ph.D. is an internationally respected psychologist, author, seminar leader and consultant. A business trial consultant for nearly 20 years, Dr. Nelson works closely with attorneys, management and corporate executives.

Dr. Nelson's books for the legal profession are A Winning Case (Prentice Hall) and Connecting With Your Client (American Bar Association). In Winning! Using Lawyers' Courtroom Techniques to Get Your Way in Everyday Situations (Prentice Hall; Get Your Way, paperback edition), Dr. Nelson explains how to use the persuasion techniques of successful trial attorneys in everyday situations.

Dr. Nelson has appeared on national and international radio and television including: CBS's "The Early Show," ABC's "The View," Fox News and CNN. She has been interviewed, quoted or written about in publications including Entrepreneur Magazine, Inc., Investor's Business Daily and Bottom Line/Personal. Dr. Nelson has spoken on appreciation techniques before audiences in the U.S., Canada and Australia.

Dr. Nelson holds advanced degrees in clinical psychology from the United States International University (M.A., Ph.D.), and sociology degrees from the University of California at Los Angeles (B.A.) and the Sorbonne, Paris (Maitrise, Doctorat 3eme Cycle). She is a member of the National Honor Society of Psychology, the American Society of Trial Consultants and the American Psychological Association.

If you'd like to learn more about the Power of Appreciation, or Dr. Noelle Nelson's other books and tapes, the following are available on www.powerofappreciationinbusiness.com. Please visit the "Store."

The Power of Appreciation: the Key to a Vibrant Life   [book]

The Power of Appreciation in Everyday Life: Appreciation Tools and Techniques for the Challenges of Daily Life

The Power of Appreciation [audiobook]

The Power of Appreciation in Business: How An Obsession With Value Increases Performance, Productivity And Profits [book]

Walk the Appreciator's Labyrinth to Health and Longevity [DVD]

The Amazing Power of Appreciation at Home, at Work, in Love [DVD]

Everyday Miracles [book]

Dangerous Relationships [book]

Winning! Using Lawyers' Courtroom Techniques to Get Your Way in Everyday Situations [book]

Winner Takes All [book]

Connecting with Your Client [book]

A Winning Case [book]

How to Give a Good Deposition and Testify Well in Court [DVD]